Nicolas Barber

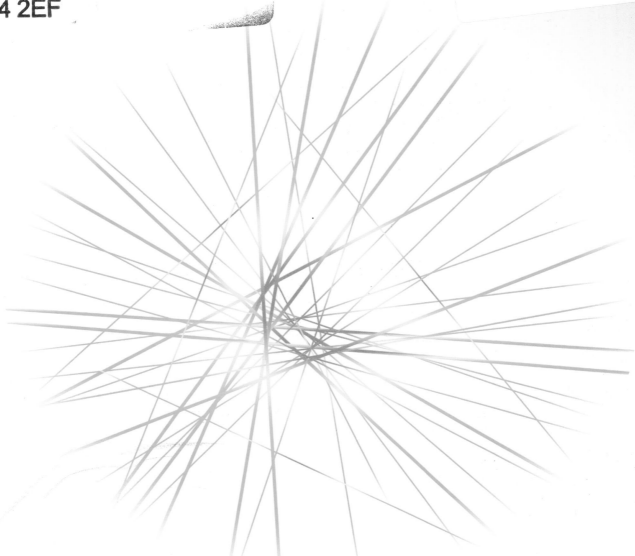

ESSENTIALS

Year 7
KS3 English
Coursebook

How to Use this Coursebook

A Note to the Teacher

This is the first of three English coursebooks for students in Key Stage 3. Together, the coursebooks for Years 7, 8 and 9 provide full coverage of the programme of study for Key Stage 3 English.

Each coursebook comprises…
- clear, concise content appropriate to that year
- questions and tasks to reinforce students' learning and help improve their confidence.

This coursebook is split into 12 topics. The first pages of a topic contain the content. They feature…
- **key words** picked out in colour in the text and listed in a box at the end of each topic
- a **Quick Test** to test understanding.

The final three pages in a topic contain questions and exercises to provide skills practice and reinforce students' understanding:
- **Key Words Exercise** – requires students to match the Key Words to their definitions.
- **Testing Understanding** – comprises a literacy exercise.
- **Skills Practice** – devoted to a relevant task to develop the students' English skills.

A pull-out answer book is included in the centre of this book. It contains the answers to the questions in the Quick Tests and to the practice sections of this coursebook.

Each coursebook is supported by a workbook for further practice and learning.

A Note to the Student

We're sure you'll enjoy using this coursebook, but follow these helpful hints to make the most of it:
- Make sure you understand the key words before moving on. These words include technical terms that you should be able to understand and use correctly, plus words that will help to expand and develop your vocabulary. If you don't understand them, look back at the context in which they're used to gain a sense of their meaning, ask your teacher or use a dictionary.
- Try to write in Standard English, use correct punctuation and good sentence construction. Read what you have written to make sure it makes sense. Some questions require extra research, using dictionaries, encyclopedias and thesauruses, or the internet.

- The tick boxes on the Contents page let you track your progress: put a tick in each box when you're confident that you know the topic.
- The questions marked with a light bulb symbol (💡) are included to help you focus on different aspects of the text. No answers are included. Instead, we suggest you write down your answers and discuss your ideas in pairs, in a small group or with your teacher.
- For many of the skills practice and extension questions, there is no right or wrong answer. Once you have your answer, refer back to the original question and make sure you have covered all the points, then ask a classmate or teacher to read your answer. Ask them questions to find out if you have communicated your ideas effectively.

Contents

Personal Writing

What is Covered in this Topic?

This topic looks at...
- some of the features of a personal profile
- how to create a factual account
- the use of opinion
- how to write for a real audience.

All About Me

This is an example of a **personal profile** from a **social networking** website. You can put your details into a page, send messages to other members and make new friends.

Other people will get an idea of what you're like from...
- the information you decide to include
- the way you describe yourself.

Mybook.com

Robbie

..is having to do his English homework (updated 2 minutes ago)

Name: Robbie Fulks

Birthday: 29th September

Interests: Aeroplanes, sport, music and reading.

What I did today

Today I was given loads of English homework by my teacher – it wasn't even homework night on the timetable, but he said that it would be good for us! I've also got loads of Science and Maths to do and I've got to get my ingredients for Food Tech for tomorrow. I won't be able to watch the football on the telly or go on MSN!

Messageboard

 Rob, are you playing against Martyrs United tomorrow?

Grant

 Have you done your Maths homework? It's solid!

Mike

 I won't be in school tomorrow. Can you tell me what I miss?

Gerald

About me

My name is Robbie and I'm from somewhere in Europe. I'm a pretty ordinary person of my age and like doing the usual stuff like watching footy, chatting with mates and relaxing.

I get bored if I have too much work to do. I'd much rather be out playing football with my mates Grant, Mike and Gerald. Mike is in the year above us at school but he's a laugh.

I have a brother who I don't see very often because he's away at University, which means I get his room – Yay!

My likes

I'm a big fan of Port Vale FC. They're in Division One but they haven't been doing very well lately. I support my local team because I can go and see them with my dad. I can't go and see Premiership teams because they are too far away from where I live.

I also like junk food! My school gives us healthy food so I can only have chips once a week, which is horrible. I would eat chips every day if I could. My mum says that would give me spots, though, which would be bad...

My top ten facts

1. My name is Robbie, but I answer to 'Rob'.
2. I have no pets.
3. I am strange because I like school.
4. I am learning to play the guitar.
5. I am very tall for my age.
6. My favourite singer is Kate Rusby.
7. I like foreign holidays. I have been to America and Holland (twice).
8. My brother has a weird name.
9. His name is Jubal.
10. I once ate a whole loaf of bread on my own.

Features of a Personal Profile

Personal profiles are all different, but they share similar features:
- Name / title.
- Personal information.
- Sections and headings.

- They are usually written in an **informal style**.
- They may contain photos, pictures, music and / or videos.

💡 *Which of these features can you see in Robbie's profile?*

Know Your Audience

When you put together your personal profile you will need to think about who might see it – your **audience**.

You need to ask yourself some questions:
- Who do you want to read it, and who else might read it?
- Why are you writing it? Is it to let your friends know more about you, or to make new friends?
- What are you going to include in your profile?

Look at Robbie's profile again. He wanted his profile to be read by his friends and also to help make some new friends.

💡 *Which parts of his profile were meant to be read by his friends? How can you tell?*

💡 *Which parts of his profile might be to attract new friends? How can you tell?*

Being Safe

You need to be careful about the information that you put online because you don't know who might read it.

The reason why you're writing it may not be the reason why someone else is reading it.

You need to be careful about what you write so that you don't give information out that someone else might use for bad reasons.

💡 *Look at Robbie's profile again – is there anything that you would tell him to take out? Why?*

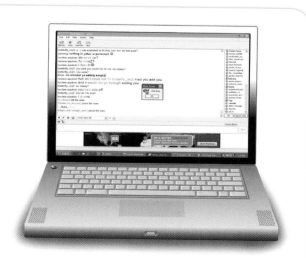

Personal Writing

The Content of Profiles

The content of a profile...
- is mainly **factual**
- may include **opinions**.

Why do you think the content is mainly going to be factual?

Why might your profile be boring if you don't include opinions?

Look at these extracts from Robbie's profile. The parts highlighted in red are facts and the parts in blue are opinions.

I'm a big fan of Port Vale FC. They're in Division One but they haven't been doing very well lately. I support my local team because I can go and see them with my dad. I can't go and see Premiership teams because they are too far away from where I live.

I also like junk food! My school gives us healthy food so I can only have chips once a week, which is horrible. I would eat chips every day if I could. My mum says that would give me spots, though, which would be bad...

Quick Test

Complete the sentences below.
1. Headings are used because...
2. Don't put your full name on a web page profile because...
3. Use a mixture of facts and opinions about yourself because...
4. Give reasons for your opinions because...
5. Lists of facts are useful because...

KEY WORDS
Make sure you understand these words before moving on!
- Social networking
- Personal profile
- Informal style
- Audience
- Factual
- Opinion

Key Words Exercise

For each question, select the correct option to complete the sentence.

1 Social networking means...
  a) mixing with other people and making new contacts
  b) removing your information from a web page
  c) being careful
  d) working out how to use a computer properly.

2 A personal profile is a...
  a) website
  b) collection of facts and opinions about you
  c) form that you fill in
  d) booklet.

3 Informal style means...
  a) writing in a serious manner
  b) writing in a relaxed manner.

4 The audience of a piece of writing is...
  a) the people who write it
  b) the people who read it.

5 'Factual' describes...
  a) things that are made up
  b) things that are false
  c) things that can be proven
  d) things that someone has said.

6 Opinions are...
  a) always false
  b) ideas that someone has made up that are true
  c) ideas that someone has made up that may be true or false
  d) the same as facts.

Personal Writing

Here is a personal profile from the same site, but filled in by a very different person.

Mybook.com

Alex

A guitar superstar. Bow down and worship me! (updated 2 minutes ago)

Name: Alex

Birthday: 1st December

Interests: Me, me and... me! (Oh – and guitars)

What I did today

Today I learnt some new chords for the guitar. The bass player in our band is just rubbish though and couldn't play the amazing new song I wrote. Why can't he see how good my ideas are? I'll have to sack him.

About me

My name is Alex and you'd better remember it cuz I'm gonna be famous. Got no time for time wasters or posers cuz they're gonna stop me from getting to the top where I deserve to be.

I am the best guitar player for my age anywhere and anyone who doesn't agree with me is a waste of space. If you want my autograph then e-mail me and send me a fiver and then I'll post it to you if I can be bothered.

My likes

I like me because I'm great. I have loads of girls who fancy me and I'm not surprised because, well, who wouldn't?

I like playing the guitar – as you should know if you've actually bothered to pay any attention to my profile. I can't be bothered with school though. I don't need to try hard because I'm going to be famous when I grow up anyway.

Messageboard

Steven

Alex – you're sacked from the band.

Amy

How many chords do you know now? Three?

Jimi

Can I have my guitar back, please?

My top ten facts

1. I'm great
2. I'm great
3. I'm great
4. I'm great
5. I'm great
6. I'm great
7. I'm great
8. I'm great
9. I'm great
10. Did I tell you that I'm great?

Testing Understanding (cont.)

1 a) Which parts of Alex's profile are meant to be read by people he knows? Explain your answer.

b) Which parts of his profile are intended for people who don't know him? Explain your answer.

2 a) Find two examples of slang in Alex's profile and write them down.

b) What impression does his use of slang create?

3 Find three examples of facts and three examples of opinions in Alex's profile.

4 Now compare Alex's profile to Robbie's.

a) Which features do the two profiles have in common?

b) How are the two profiles different?

c) What do these differences tell us about Alex?

d) Does Alex give more or fewer opinions than Robbie?

e) Does Robbie appear more or less reasonable than Alex? Explain your answer.

5 Which of the two boys would you most like to be friends with? Explain your answer.

Skills Practice

Now that you know what a personal profile is like, have a go at creating your own.

Step 1: First of all, plan and decide…

- who you're going to write it for – who do you want your audience to be? Everyone? Just a few friends?
- why you are going to write it. Do you want to tell the world about your hobbies and skills? Do you just want to stay in touch with your friends?
- what you are going to include.

Step 2: Now draft your ideas – sketch them out in rough and work out what goes where. Check your spelling, punctuation and your use of slang. If you make lots of mistakes, just think what sort of impression you're going to give.

Step 3: Write up your final version. Get other people to read it and ask them whether they think it gives a fair impression of what you're like. Listen to their suggestions. Redraft it to make it even better.

Extension Activity

Write personal profiles for these people:

1 Your teacher – he / she wants to come across as trendy and fashionable and wants to be noticed by the general public. What would you include?

2 Your best friend – he / she wants to come across as a really nice person to the pupils at their new school. What would you include to create a good impression of them?

3 A well-known person who has a bad reputation – what would you include to change people's opinion of them?

Shakespeare

What is Covered in this Topic?

This topic looks at...
- the background to Shakespeare's theatre and drama
- how Shakespearean language is linked to modern-day language
- features of historical writing.

The Original Globe Theatre

The original Globe theatre...
- was built in 1599 in London
- was a wood-framed building, roughly circular in shape – the stage was raised by 4 to 6 feet and pillars supported the roof
- could hold between 2000 and 3000 people
- burned down in 1613 when a cannon used as an effect in *Henry VIII* set fire to it. The site was later used to build cheap housing on. **Excavations** in the 20th Century revealed the site. Part of the Globe lies under protected buildings, so further **archaeology** isn't allowed.

The Audience

- It cost one old penny to watch the plays. For two pennies, you could sit under cover in a **gallery** with a good view where other people could see you.
- Up to 1000 penny-paying **groundlings** would stand in the 'pit' in front of the stage, squashed and exposed to the weather.
- Shakespeare wrote about groundlings unkindly, saying in *Hamlet* that they could only understand simple performances.
- It was possible to buy food and drink in the theatre and if the play or the actors weren't liked, it could be thrown at them!

Performance

- Plays didn't begin as they do now – there were no lights or curtains to tell the audience that the play was starting.
- Shakespeare used several ways to get the audience's attention. For example, *Romeo and Juliet* starts with a spoken **prologue**, followed by **bawdy** jokes and a large fight.

Actors and Props

- There were very few props. They were often left on stage as there was no easy way of removing them.
- There were some stage and sound effects, such as fireworks and musical instruments.
- Actors entered the stage from the rear, where they would get ready first. They might appear from trapdoors or from above on a rope if the play demanded it.
- All parts were played by men as it was a sign of shame for a woman to act on stage.
- Teenage boys would play younger girls, but would fall out of favour or move onto other parts when their voices broke.

Inside the Globe

This diagram shows what it was like inside the Globe theatre.

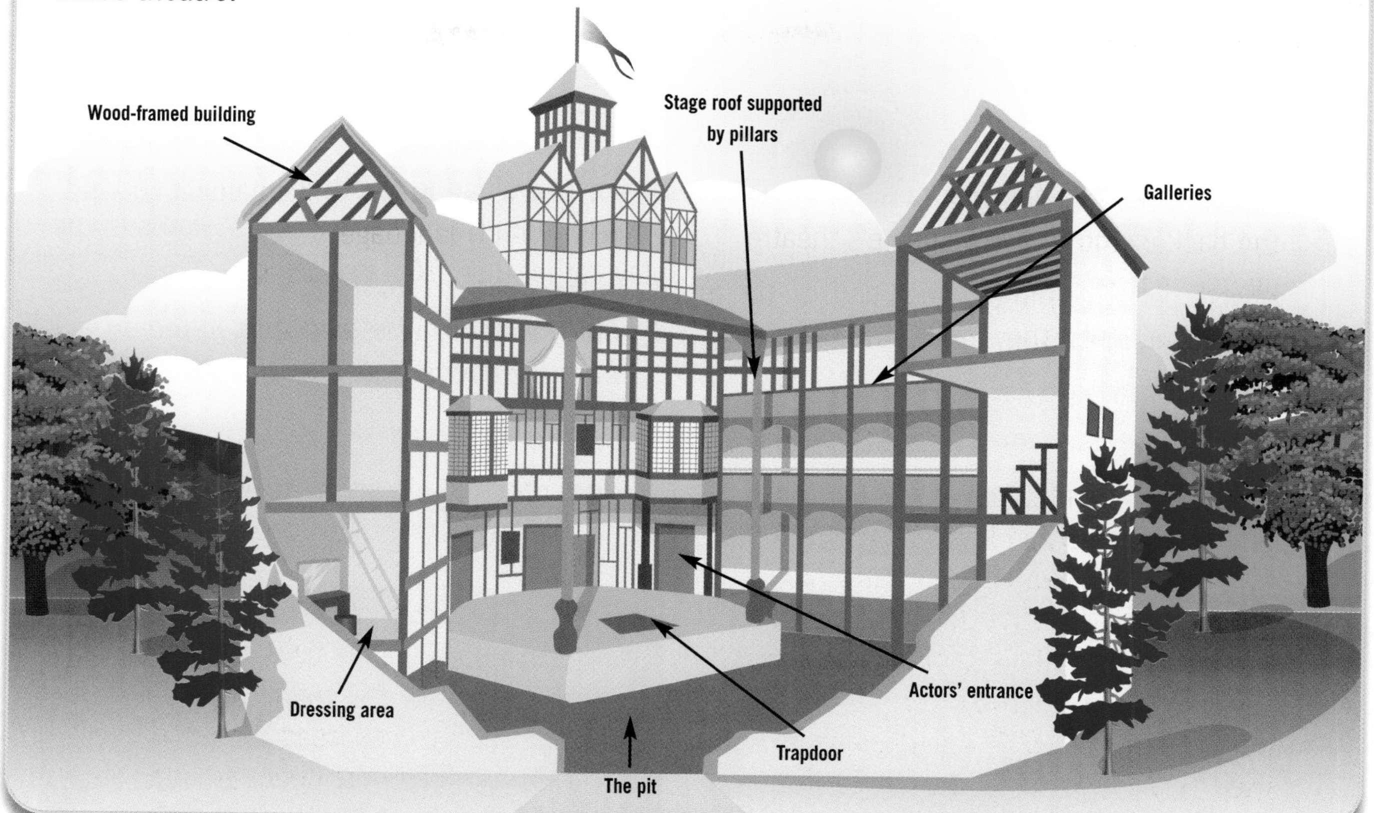

Wood-framed building

Stage roof supported by pillars

Galleries

Dressing area

The pit

Trapdoor

Actors' entrance

Eyewitness Account

Read this account by Sir Henry Wooton, written in July 1613, of the burning down of the Globe theatre.

- *From this account, what can you work out about the costumes of the actors in this play?*

- *What do you think 'certain chambers being shot off at his entry' is describing? (Clue – think of the chambers of a gun)*

- *Why didn't the audience notice the fire at first?*

Now, to let matters of state sleep, I will entertain you at the present with what happened this week at the Bankside. The King's players had a new play, called All is True, representing some principal pieces of the reign of Henry VIII, which was set forth with many extraordinary circumstances of pomp and majesty, even to the matting of the stage; the Knights of the Order with their Georges and garters, the Guards with their embroidered coats, and the like: sufficient in truth within a while to make greatness very familiar, if not ridiculous. Now, King Henry making a masque at the Cardinal Wolsey's house, and certain chambers being shot off at his entry, some of the paper, or other stuff, wherewith one of them was stopped, did light on the thatch, where being thought at first but an idle smoke, and their eyes more attentive to the show, it kindled inwardly, and ran round like a train, consuming within less than an hour the whole house to the very grounds.

Shakespeare

Macbeth

Macbeth was written and first performed, it is believed, in 1606.

Plays were performed in the open and, as there were no stage lights, they had to be performed in the daytime.

Shakespeare had to give the audience an idea of the setting from the characters' words in the play, rather than from lighting effects.

💡 *Can you see how he does this in the extract from the opening scene of Macbeth below?*

Macbeth – Act 1 Scene 1

The passage below contains words that aren't used much nowadays. For example...

- hurlyburly = confusion
- exeunt = exit
- ere = before
- anon = see you later.

	Thunder and lightning. Enter three Witches
First Witch	When shall we three meet again? In thunder, lightning, or in rain?
Second Witch	When the hurlyburly's done, When the battle's lost and won.
Third Witch	That will be ere the set of sun.
First Witch	Where the place?
Second Witch	Upon the heath.
Third Witch	There to meet with Macbeth.
First Witch	I come, Graymalkin!
Second Witch	Paddock calls.
Third Witch	Anon.
ALL	Fair is foul, and foul is fair: Hover through the fog and filthy air.
	Exeunt

💡 *Do any words in the passage have similarities with modern words, phrases or ideas?*

Modern Meaning

Some Elizabethan words Shakespeare uses are similar to modern words. The following extract shows Lady Macbeth talking about what the witches have promised her husband Macbeth, and what she feels about him.

> Glamis thou art, and Cawdor, and shalt be
> What thou art promised. Yet do I fear thy nature.
> It is too full o' the milk of human kindness
> To catch the nearest way. Thou wouldst be great;
> Art not without ambition, but without
> The illness should attend it.

Here are some more Shakespearean words and their modern meanings:

- Nature = Character.
- Milk of human kindness = Goodness.
- Catch the nearest way = Take a short cut.
- Attend = Go with.

Deciphering Shakespeare

Shakespeare often uses words that we don't use anymore. This witch's speech could be hard to understand so a copy of the play that includes a glossary or notes will be useful.

> Weary se'nnights nine times nine
> Shall he dwindle, peak, and pine;
> Though his bark cannot be lost,
> Yet it shall be tempest-toss'd.
>
> _____
>
> *Notes
> se'nnights = seven nights
> dwindle, peak, and pine = waste away in agony
> bark = ship or boat
> tempest-toss'd = thrown about by storms

 Try to translate this short speech, using the notes above.

Understanding Shakespeare

It's not too hard to understand Shakespeare if you learn about the way he writes.

Sometimes he changes word order to...
- fit a rhyme
- fit a certain number of beats / syllables
- add emphasis.

Word order is called **syntax**, so Shakespeare is changing the normal syntax.

Can you find an example of this in the Macbeth extract on page 12?

Quick Test

1. In which city was the Globe theatre found?
2. Who played all the parts in plays in Shakespeare's time?
3. What was the area called at the front of the stage where the groundlings stood?
4. What was the main way that Shakespeare helped to set the scene without lighting?

KEY WORDS
Make sure you understand these words before moving on!
- Gallery
- Groundlings
- Prologue
- Bawdy
- Excavations
- Archaeology
- Pomp
- Masque
- Thatch
- Kindled
- Syntax
- Syllables

Shakespeare

Key Words Exercise

Match each key word with its meaning.

Gallery	Rude and loud
Groundlings	The study of history through digging up the past
Prologue	Showing-off linked to well-off people
Bawdy	Changing word order
Excavations	Set fire
Archaeology	Digs done by archaeologists
Pomp	A kind of play
Masque	People who paid a penny to stand and watch a play
Thatch	Beats in a word or a line of text
Kindled	An introduction to a play before the main story begins
Syllables	Roof material made from straw
Syntax	Raised seats in the theatre

Anagrams

Use the following clues to unscramble each word:

1. Shakespeare's famous tragedy about the Prince of Denmark.   LEAMTH
2. Shakespeare's play about doomed lovers.   ORMOE DNA JULTIE
3. Shakespeare's play about an evil Scottish king.   HCAEBMT
4. Shakespeare's main theatre.   HTE BOLGE
5. In a Shakespearean theatre, this was where the covered seats were.   RLAGLEY

Testing Understanding

Are the following statements true or false?

1. The original Globe theatre was built in 1601.

2. The original Globe theatre could hold between 2000 and 3000 people.

3. The cheapest place to stand in the Globe Theatre was the pit.

4. It cost one pound to stand in the pit.

5. Plays took place at night at the original Globe.

6. *Romeo and Juliet* starts off with a love scene.

7. The Globe theatre used scenery that was moved on and off stage during the play.

8. Actors at the Globe might pop up through a trapdoor if it was needed.

9. Women played some of the best parts in Shakespeare's time.

10. Fireworks might be used in an original Globe play.

11. The original Globe burned down.

12. The last play performed at the original Globe was *Henry VIII*.

13. There are four witches in the opening scene of *Macbeth*.

14. Lady Macbeth is Macbeth's mother.

15. Shakespeare wrote in a completely different type of language to that used today.

16. A prologue would come at the end of a play.

17. Musical instruments would be used to create sound effects for the performance of Shakespeare's plays.

18. A groundling was an actor.

19. The original Globe put on performances for hundreds of years.

20. Fruit and vegetables might be thrown at the performers.

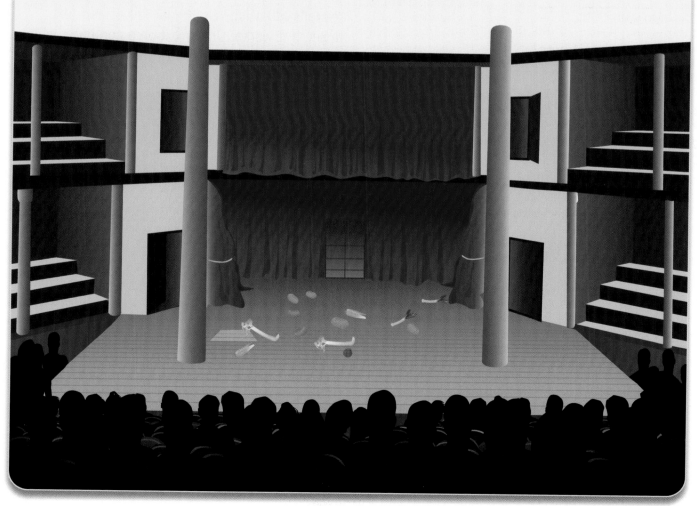

Shakespeare

Use the information in this topic to produce a guide to Shakespeare's original Globe theatre. Your guide must be aimed at tourists who don't know much about the theatre. It should be 250-300 words long and might include pictures.

Step 1: Your audience consists of tourists. How will this affect the information that you include?

How much detail will they need? Are all tourists the same, or should you consider the different kinds of tourists who might be interested in the original Globe?

How will the fact that you're writing for some people who don't know much about the original Globe affect...
- your choice of vocabulary?
- your style – formal or informal, or a mixture of both?
- the amount of detail you include?

Step 2: Look through the topic and make a list of information you think would be interesting to tourists. Make a list in order of importance and number it so that 1 = the most important.

Step 3: Do a word count of what you've included in your list. Do you think you have the right amount of information? If you have too much information, use the order of importance you have made to remove some things at the bottom of your list. If you haven't got enough, look at what else you could add.

Step 4: How are you going to organise your information? Sort it into paragraphs or sections based on topics. For example, if you have three points about what the theatre looked like, put them all in the same section or paragraph.

Step 5: Decide what pictures you might use and where you will put them so that they fit with the text. What pictures would grab the reader's attention? Draft your layout and text to see if it works. Drafting it on a computer will help you to play around with the order to see what works best.

Extension Activity

Rewrite the guide for a different audience – for example, Year 4 pupils. What would you do differently and why?

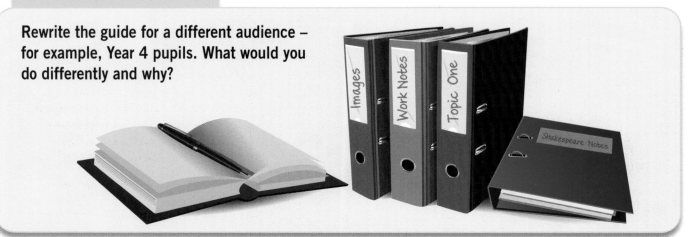

Genre & Science Fiction

What is Covered in this Topic?

This topic looks at...
- what is meant by 'genre'
- how to spot and use features of science fiction and other genres.

What does Genre Mean?

According to a dictionary definition, 'genre' means:

*A category of artistic **composition**, as in music or literature, marked by a **distinctive** style, **form**, or content.*

There are lots of different genres of writing, for example, horror, crime, romance, comedy, epic, and historical.

Mixing Genres

Stories would be boring if they all had the same features.

Writers try to make their stories more interesting and original by mixing features of more than one genre.

Mixing genres can help to make the story less predictable.

💡 *This passage contains a mixture of at least two genres. Can you work out what genres this passage is written in? What features tell you this?*

> The fair isle of Berwyn was a lonely, single peak that rose defiantly out of the distant ocean, a land well-known for its magically gifted people. From its narrow valleys and gloomy, mist-filled villages and hamlets, many Acadians had set off to seek the rulers of the seas and to seek employment as an advisor, politician or even a wizard-like mage. Others would go exploring, hoping to find parts of the lost seas that no man had seen before. According to folklore, the most fearsome voyager was a man who went by the name of Fulksar...

Different Genres

The following extracts are examples of different genres.

💡 *What features help you to identify the genre of each extract?*

> Dirk Clayton looked down the long, dusty street and watched the tumbleweed roll across, occasionally hitting the cacti that clung between the saloons and dime stores. From the distant end of the street came the thudding sound of a horse's hooves. A dark figure gradually rode into view, the rider wearing mud-encrusted chaps, leather boots and a Stetson hat pulled down over the eyes.
>
> 'Howdy,' came the deep, dull voice. 'Have you seen the Sheriff? I got a score to settle...'

Genre & Science Fiction

Different Genres (cont.)

Colorado Smith adjusted his hat and flicked off the sweat – the jungle heat was getting to him now, but he couldn't give up. In the faint distance came the sound of the chanting tribesmen, tracking his every move. Every twig that he stepped on was a clue to where he was. Would they reach the Golden Statue of Sullaria before he did? If they did, then the fate of the world was in doubt. He had to get there first. He moved on, slipping, sliding and gliding through the dense undergrowth, racing and panting towards the distant mountain where the golden prize awaited him.

The dark door hid a deadly secret. Slowly it creaked open and a small draught found its way towards Barry's face. Strange thoughts raced through his mind about the legends that had grown about that room, about people who had disappeared when entering there and who'd never been seen again. Would he be joining that group, or would the precautions he'd taken be enough? He gripped the gun at his waist tightly, took a nervous step forward and headed into the misty gloom.

'Mission control to Dallas Wayne. Do you receive me?' The hum of the ship's engines was the only sound in the darkness of space. Where before there was the chatter of the crew, now there was nothing. A few lights blinked and spluttered automatically. A hollow grinding interrupted the calm.

The mothership had docked. Stars twinkled peacefully, forming a strangely calm background to what they were about to find within. The docking bay snapped open and the sound of human movement disturbed the emptiness. But it wasn't empty. Something was waiting.

Holly looked across the room and gazed longingly at the dark, handsome figure opposite. He stood tall and strong, confidently talking to one of his colleagues. She wished that she could dare to go and talk to him, but she didn't have a reason or an excuse and felt that she would make a fool of herself if she did. He slowly turned, as if he knew she was watching. His face broke into a grin and he winked knowingly in her direction. Holly's heart skipped as she realised that the grin was aimed at her – she blushed a deep crimson and coughed nervously. How did he know that she existed? She was only the girl who made the tea and he was the big man in the boardroom…

Science Fiction

Writing in a certain genre will contain features that are common across a variety of similar types of story.

In science fiction, you might find that...
- stories are set in the future
- stories ask the question, 'What if...?'
- some stories consider an **alternative** view of history
- unusual **technology** is involved
- aliens, space travel or other worlds are involved.

Can you see any of these features in the passage from The War of the Worlds?

THE WAR OF THE WORLDS

The end of the cylinder was being screwed out from within. Nearly two feet of shining screw projected. Somebody blundered against me, and I narrowly missed being pitched onto the top of the screw. I turned, and as I did so the screw must have come out, for the lid of the cylinder fell upon the gravel with a ringing concussion.

I stuck my elbow into the person behind me, and turned my head towards the Thing again. For a moment that circular cavity seemed perfectly black. I had the sunset in my eyes.

I think everyone expected to see a man emerge – possibly something a little unlike us terrestrial men, but in all essentials a man. I know I did. But, looking, I presently saw something stirring within the shadow: greyish billowy movements, one above another, and then two luminous disks – like eyes. Then something

resembling a little grey snake, about the thickness of a walking stick, coiled up out of the writhing middle, and wriggled in the air towards me – and then another. I heard inarticulate exclamations on all sides.

There was a general movement backwards. I saw the shopman struggling still on the edge of the pit. I found myself alone, and saw the people on the other side of the pit running off, Stent among them. I looked again at the cylinder, and ungovernable terror gripped me. I stood petrified and staring.

A big greyish rounded bulk, the size, perhaps, of a bear, was rising slowly and painfully out of the cylinder. As it bulged up and caught the light, it glistened like wet leather. Two large dark-coloured eyes were regarding me steadfastly. The mass that framed them, the head of the thing, was rounded, and had, one might say, a face. There was a mouth under the eyes, the lipless brim of which quivered and panted, and dropped saliva. The whole creature heaved and pulsated convulsively. A lank tentacular appendage gripped the edge of the cylinder, another swayed in the air.

An example of Science Fiction writing, from *The War of the Worlds* by H.G. Wells.

Genre & Science Fiction

Science Fiction Language

To make the story more interesting, science fiction uses…
- well-chosen detail
- similes and metaphors
- adjectives
- short sentences to shock
- lexis (choice of words) of fear.

Can you find at least one example of each in the extract from The War of the Worlds on page 19?

A genre will typically contain words to do with its style, in order to create the mood of that genre.

Which of the words in the table below might you find in science fiction writing? They might all appear in a story, but which are most typical of the genre?

rocket	cyber	heat
universe	planet	sky
flower	space	expression
galactic	ground	UFO
metallic	calm	legs
robot	heat	alien
darkness	male	horse

ALIENS SUCKED **OUT HIS BRAINS!**
thenews

Quick Test

1. Are there only different genres in literature?
2. Which genre deals with the question 'What if…?'
3. Can you have a mixture of genres in one piece of writing?
4. Does writing in a genre guarantee that it is interesting?
5. What problem is there if a writer sticks too closely to the features of a genre?

KEY WORDS
Make sure you understand these words before moving on!
- Composition
- Distinctive
- Form
- Mage
- Dense
- Cylinder
- Concussion
- Cavity
- Inarticulate
- Ungovernable
- Steadfastly
- Pulsated
- Appendage
- Alternative
- Technology

Key Words Exercise

The lists below contain 15 words and 20 meanings, so 5 of the meanings don't match any of the words. Match each word with its meaning.

Word	Meaning
Composition	Thick
Distinctive	Thin
Form	Not very clearly spoken
Cylinder	A round, tube-shaped container
Concussion	A kind of wizard
Cavity	Shape or structure
Inarticulate	A robot
Ungovernable	Clear and having definite characteristics
Steadfastly	Something that has been composed or created
Pulsated	The state of being stunned
Appendage	A hole
Alternative	A bat
Technology	Throbbed
Mage	Jumped
Dense	Something added on
	A different way of doing something
	Not possible to control
	With determination
	Equipment or machinery designed to do a job
	Rubber boots

Genre & Science Fiction

Testing Understanding

Choose the correct options in the following sentences.

1. Genre is a word that describes the particular *style / author / cover* of a piece of writing or other *film / music / composition*. All genres have their own *authors / comments / features*, which help the *author / reader / writer* to identify them. In science fiction, for example, the text will include references to such things as *castles / adventure / future technology*.

2. Different genres contain different features. Romance stories will contain *dreamy / scary / mysterious* descriptive words, whereas cowboy stories might contain references to *ships and the sea / jungles and gold / horses and guns*.

3. It can get *boring / interesting* if writers stick too closely to the features of one genre in their story. To get round this, writers often *lose / use* features of more than one genre to make their story more *clever / original / dull*.

4. Using the features of a genre will give your story a top *grade / style / boost* but it won't make it interesting unless you describe those features well. You will need to also include *appropriate / big* words to develop your style.

5. Using descriptive techniques, which includes *punctuation / adjectives* and *similes / paragraphs*, is very important.

True or False?

Here are some statements about features of different genres. Which of the statements are true and which are false?

1. You can't mix features of different genres.

2. The science fiction genre doesn't have to contain references to aliens.

3. Historical romance is a genre.

4. In examples of the mystery genre you will always find detectives and policemen.

5. In the romance genre, you will always have a happy ending.

6. You can mix historical features and science fiction in the same story.

7. A romance story might have a cowboy in it.

8. Using features of a genre doesn't guarantee better writing.

9. In adventure stories, the heroes are never women.

10. Using well-chosen adjectives will improve your writing, no matter what the genre.

TRUE OR FALSE?

356

Write a science fiction story that includes the ideas listed below:

OUTER SPACE

ALIENS

A Distant Planet

NEW TECHNOLOGY

Futuristic-Sounding Names

People from Earth

A Battle between Aliens and Earth people

a cliffhanger or twist at the end

IT MUST BE SET IN THE FUTURE

Step 1: Decide the order of events in your story. Work out how and where you're going to include the ideas given here. This will be your outline plan.

Step 2: To make your story more interesting, you will need to find ways of describing the features. Use a thesaurus to come up with lists of adjectives and adverbs to describe the main features and events in your plan. If you know how to create similes and metaphors, these would be good to use too.

Step 3: The most important part of your story is the opening; you need to grab the reader's attention or they will not read on. Make sure you have a well-chosen description in your first couple of lines – use the techniques described in step 2.

Step 4: The next most important parts are the ending and the key events – make sure you use plenty of descriptions to make these parts stand out, like H.G. Wells does in *The War of the Worlds*. After you have done that, start to draft the whole story.

Step 5: When you have completed your draft, let someone else read it. Listen to their suggestions for improvements – can they spot the features of the genre? Which parts work well? Which parts could do with more work? Redraft it before finally completing your science fiction masterpiece!

The Writer's Craft

What is Covered in this Topic?

This topic looks at…
- descriptive techniques
- how to use words more effectively
- how to use descriptive techniques to make writing more interesting
- how to develop original similes and metaphors.

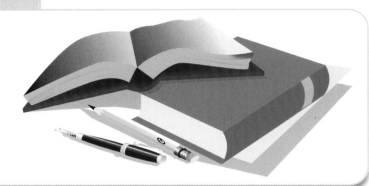

The Way You Write

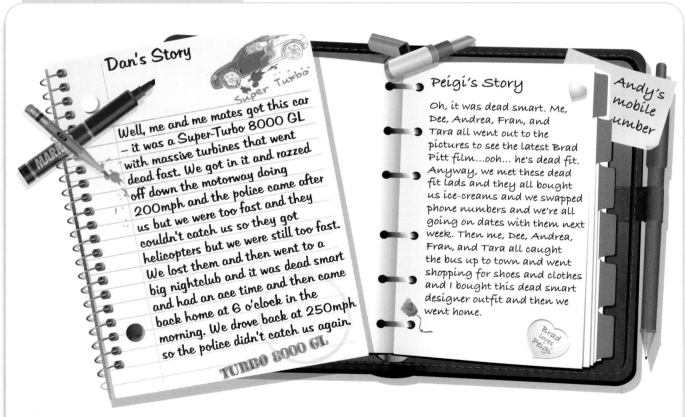

It's not just what you write, but how you write it that's important. Here are two examples of writing. They may not have the effect the writers intended them to have!

Dan clearly enjoyed writing his story, but he wanted to make it sound mean and tough when it actually sounds funny and silly.

Where do you think Dan went wrong?

Like Dan, Peigi is obviously writing about something she enjoyed, but she's made the same mistake as Dan, which is IT'S NOT WHAT YOU WRITE BUT THE WAY YOU WRITE IT THAT MATTERS!

Writing Techniques

A good writer uses descriptive techniques. Using original versions of the following techniques will improve your writing further.

Adjective – a word that describes and adds extra information to a noun. For example, 'Henry always wore *dark* clothes.'

Simile – a comparison that generally uses 'as' or 'like'. For example, 'Henry's dark clothes made him look as *gloomy as a broken lightbulb*.'

Metaphor – a comparison where one thing is given the qualities of something else. For example, 'Henry *was a pit of gloom after realising he had failed his SATs*.'

Similes

The following similes are common:
- Deaf as a post.
- Solid as a rock.
- As different as chalk and cheese.
- As quiet as a mouse.
- As wise as an owl.

Common similes aren't as effective because they're overused and don't put a precise picture in the reader's mind.

You don't have to think of a totally original simile to develop your writing, although it helps if you can. You might begin with common similes to help you develop into writing original ones.

The Writer's Craft

Developing Common Similes

Here are some more common similes:
- As pale as a ghost.
- As blind as a bat.

To improve these similes, you can add an adjective or adjectives before the final noun. For example…
- as pale as a painted ghost
- as blind as a hooded bat.

To improve them further you might add an extra **clause** – extra information in the form of a phrase – after the main simile:
- As pale as a painted ghost, who's been faded by sunlight.
- As blind as a hooded bat, that's been locked in a darkened cell.

Try to improve the following similes by adding extra adjectives and clauses.
- *As quiet as a mouse.*
- *As wise as an owl.*

◦ LIBRARY– QUIET PLEASE ◦

Making Metaphors

Metaphors are a more powerful way of describing events in a story's opening or ending, or at important moments in the story.

Look at the difference between these two sentences:

Simile	Donna was as scared as a timid, trembling mouse, hiding from a fearsome cat.
Metaphor	Donna was a scared, timid, trembling mouse, hiding from a fearsome cat.

The metaphor is stronger because it's not saying Donna is 'like' the mouse – it's saying she 'is' the mouse, so it has a more powerful effect on the reader.

Notice how the same ideas have been used in the simile and the metaphor. By taking the words 'as' or 'like' out of a simile, you can make a metaphor.

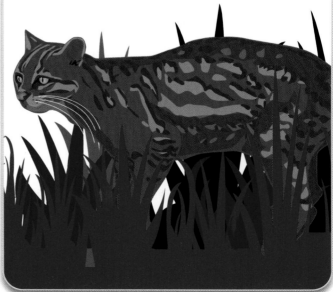

Sound Effects

Alliteration is the repetition of the same letters or sounds at the start of words that are close together. For example, 'The <u>cr</u>acked, <u>cr</u>azy footpath <u>cr</u>umbled beneath his feet.'

Alliteration should be used sparingly – only when you want the sounds of the letters to create a feeling, or perhaps to copy the sound of something.

Onomatopoeia is when words sound like the things they're describing, for example, 'moo', 'crack' and 'plop'.

Onomatopoeia should be used sparingly, for sound effects. If you overdo it, your writing could end up sounding cartoon-like and immature.

Assonance – the repetition of similar or identical vowel sounds, for example, 'R<u>ou</u>gh, t<u>ou</u>gh <u>u</u>ncl<u>u</u>ttered st<u>u</u>ff.'

This is similar to alliteration in the way that you should use it – for example, to emphasise a feeling or a sound effect.

Personification and Pathetic Fallacy

Personification is when you apply human qualities to something that isn't human, or is **abstract**. For example…
- the chair rocked back on its heels (The chair is described as though it's acting like a human)
- fear wrote its name in their hearts (Fear is being described as though it's a person).

Pathetic fallacy is a form of personification, but one where you give human qualities to something in nature. For example, 'The sky cried.'

Personification and pathetic fallacy are good techniques that make your descriptions more powerful. They can have the same strong impact as metaphors.

Quick Test

1. Complete these common similes:
   As cold as i…; As flat as a p…; As hard as n…
2. What do you call a comparison that uses 'as' or 'like'?
3. What do you call a comparison where one thing is said to be another?
4. What do you call words that are positioned close together and begin with the same letter or sound?
5. What is onomatopoeia?
6. Convert this simile into a metaphor:
   Tara was as nervous as a trembling child at the dentist's.

KEY WORDS
Make sure you understand these words before moving on!
- Adjective
- Simile
- Metaphor
- Clause
- Alliteration
- Onomatopoeia
- Assonance
- Personification
- Abstract
- Pathetic fallacy

The Writer's Craft

Match each keyword with its definition.

Adjective	A comparison where one thing is said to be another.
Simile	A group of words close together that begin with the same letter or sound.
Metaphor	Repeated use of similar or identical vowel sounds, in words that are close together.
Clause	A phrase that forms part or all of a sentence.
Alliteration	A kind of metaphor where abstract or non-human things are given human qualities.
Onomatopoeia	A word that describes a noun.
Assonance	Not real – an idea or concept.
Personification	A comparison using 'as' or 'like'.
Pathetic fallacy	A word that sounds like the thing it's describing.
Abstract	A kind of metaphor where things from nature are given human qualities.

Comprehension

Choose the correct options in the following sentences.

1. If you use *an adjective / onomatopoeia / assonance* to describe a noun, it will add extra detail to it and tell the reader more about it.

2. If you add a *simile / metaphor / adjective* to a description by comparing, using 'as' or 'like', you will put a picture in the reader's mind, which will help them to understand what you're describing.

3. A *simile / metaphor / adjective* is also a comparison, but stronger in its effect because it's saying that one thing is another.

as...   like...

Testing Understanding

Read the diary extract below and find all the examples of the following techniques.

1. Alliteration
2. Adjectives
3. Similes
4. Metaphors
5. Personification
6. Pathetic fallacy
7. Assonance

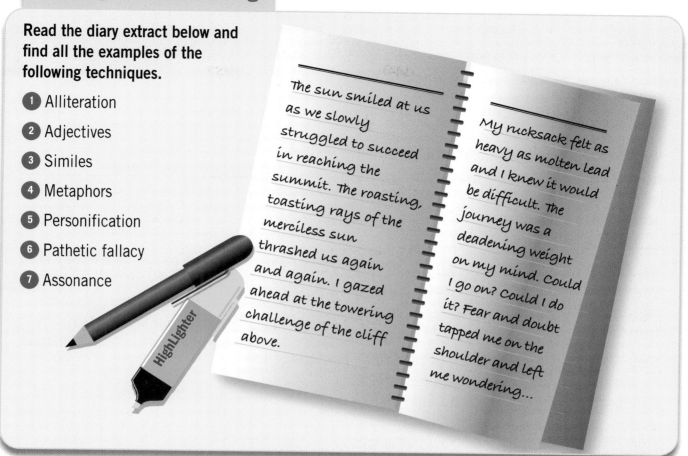

The sun smiled at us as we slowly struggled to succeed in reaching the summit. The roasting, toasting rays of the merciless sun thrashed us again and again. I gazed ahead at the towering challenge of the cliff above.

My rucksack felt as heavy as molten lead and I knew it would be difficult. The journey was a deadening weight on my mind. Could I go on? Could I do it? Fear and doubt tapped me on the shoulder and left me wondering...

Techniques

Name the techniques used in the following sentences.

1. The moon smiled down at us as we walked in its light.

2. His mood was as heavy as a lorry-load of bricks.

3. The mad, bad dad ran through the sand.

4. The rugged, rough, ramshackle cottage was finally theirs.

5. The desk did a back-flip and landed on Lisa's foot.

6. Boom! Crack! The ship exploded, disintegrated and sank.

7. The smooth, silky structure was as unreal as a dream.

8. Glug... Kelli deftly drank the delightful drink.

The Writer's Craft

Skills Practice

Write a description using the techniques in this topic. Using a thesaurus will help you find a wider range of descriptive words. If you have internet access, there's a site called www.thesaurus.com

Step 1: Describe the room you're in. It's a good way to start because you won't get carried away. Make a list of what's in the room, all the objects and people. Note what you can see from the room.

Step 2: Organise your ideas into paragraphs. For example, you might have one paragraph on furniture and another on the view from the window. When you've done this, decide on an order. You might want to order your paragraphs by their importance to you, or by the order you see them when entering the room.

Step 3: Look at each paragraph. What techniques could you use to create descriptions of objects, views, etc.? If they have a texture or make a sound, you might use alliteration, assonance or onomatopoeia.

If you want to create a picture in the reader's mind, then use similes, metaphors, personification or pathetic fallacy. Use plenty of adjectives. Develop your ideas individually and then build up your overall description from small parts.

Step 4: When you've drafted your ideas, read them out loud. How well do they link together? Do you need more connectives to link your ideas? Have you used similar techniques too often, or too close together? If you have, redraft until you get the result you want.

Extension Activity

Choose either Dan or Peigi's story at the start of this topic on page 24. Keep to the same facts, but rewrite the story using a range of descriptive techniques to make it more interesting for the person who reads it.

More Writer's Craft

What is Covered in this Topic?

This topic looks at...
- ways to make your writing more descriptive using verbs and adverbs
- how to vary sentences
- how to target parts of your writing to achieve the best effect.

Verbs and Adverbs

A **verb** is a word that **indicates** an action, such as 'run', 'wait ' or 'snore'. Verbs are often referred to as 'doing' words.

The sign of a good writer is more to do with their choice of verbs than adjectives. The following passage uses unadventurous verbs that don't tell the reader much about the character or events:

> Effin <u>ran</u> to the shops but <u>walked</u> the last few yards. He <u>walked</u> into the shop and <u>got</u> some food. He <u>put</u> it in his bag and <u>went</u> home.

By choosing more unusual verbs, you grab the reader's attention. The choice of verbs starts to create a more exciting story:

> Effin <u>raced</u> to the shops but <u>strolled</u> the last few yards. He <u>ambled</u> into the shop and <u>stole</u> some food. He <u>stuffed</u> it in his bag and <u>sprinted</u> home.

💡 *Can you think of verbs to improve the following passage? Is your version more interesting than the original?*

Andy got out of bed and walked into the kitchen. He got a cup out of the cupboard and made a cup of tea. He touched his head because it hurt.

Adding Adverbs

Adverbs are words that describe how you do something i.e. they describe verbs. They often end in 'ly', but not always – examples include 'quickly', 'lazily' and 'fast'. In a passage that contains a lot of action, using adverbs is a good technique because they describe what's happening in greater detail.

Compare this passage to the versions above.

> Effin raced <u>quickly</u> to the shops but strolled <u>lazily</u> over the last few yards. He ambled <u>nervously</u> into the shop and <u>secretly</u> stole some food. He <u>quickly</u> <u>stuffed</u> it in his bag and sprinted home <u>speedily</u>.

More Writer's Craft

Finding Verbs and Adverbs

Look at this passage from *Buddy* by Nigel Hinton. At this point, Buddy and his friends have just peeped through the door of a derelict house and have seen something spooky and unexplained.

💡 *What verbs can you find? Think about what they have in common and what feelings they create?*

💡 *Why do you think Nigel Hinton only uses two adverbs in this passage?*

> Charmian screamed and together they flew down the steps in terror. Dashing across the gravel Charmian tripped over the edge of the lawn. She crashed against Buddy and they both fell onto the wet grass. They stumbled up and ran blindly towards the gate. Buddy banged his elbow as he squeezed through, and a half-sob, half-laugh, shook him. His legs felt weak with the pain and the panic but he forced himself to run. Charmian could hardly keep up with him but he grabbed her hand and pulled her after him.

Positioning Adverbs

The adverb doesn't always have to come before the verb that it's describing.

The **positioning** of the adverb can come in the following places:

1. At the start of the sentence – 'Quickly, Bob caught the train after work to get to the theatre'.
2. After the verb – 'Bob caught the train quickly after work to get to the theatre'.
3. Before the verb – 'Bob quickly caught the train after work to get to the theatre'.

You can create different effects and emphasis by placing the adverb in different places. The first version above seems hurried. The second one makes the act of catching the train more important, whereas the last one makes Bob seem more important!

💡 *The following sentences have the verbs underlined:*

1. *Holway <u>ran</u> to the camera shop.*
2. *Kristina <u>dug</u> the plants in her back garden.*
3. *Ed <u>used</u> the video camera to <u>film</u> the band.*
4. *Preston <u>watched</u> his dad <u>performing</u> at the show.*
5. *Andrea <u>yawned</u> when she <u>walked</u> into the room.*

Add your own adverb, either before or after each verb, to make the sentences more interesting.

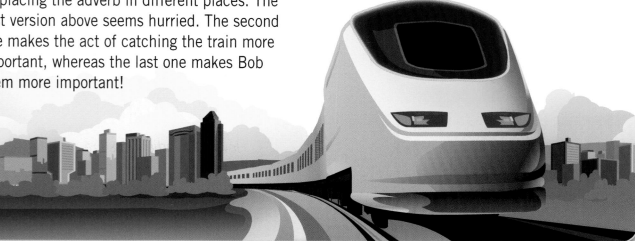

Word Order

Changing the word order can affect the tone and effect of a sentence. This works best with **complex** sentences and some **compound** ones.

For example...

- 'Will didn't want to go back home, because it was raining and it was too far to travel' – the main clause is first, suggesting it's the most important thing in the sentence.
- 'Because it was raining and too far to travel, Will didn't want to go back home' – the main clause is at the end, suggesting that the reasons in the sentence are more important.
- 'Will, because it was raining and too far to travel, didn't want to go back home' – the main clause is split in two, suggesting that all parts of the sentence are of roughly equal importance.

💡 *Try reordering the following sentences with either the main clause at the end or a split main clause.*

1. *Lisa didn't want to leave the house, because it was cold and she was ill.*
2. *Michelle bought the presents early, as it was Christmas and she was well organised.*
3. *Emma didn't like her photograph, because of the bad lighting and the spot on her nose.*
4. *Rachel ran the marathon, despite getting blisters and a leg injury the previous time.*
5. *Silvana ate the pizza, although it was dry and she didn't like the taste.*

Writing for Effect

A good writer chooses when and where to use a particular technique to create the best effect. All writers focus on...

- openings
- endings
- key moments.

The writers of the three extracts in the following section have chosen techniques carefully to achieve the effects that they wanted to place in the readers' minds. As a good writer, you will need to do the same.

Creating Imagery

John Steinbeck uses lots of adjectives to create a vivid, almost photographic, picture to get the reader's attention in the opening of *Of Mice and Men*.

A few miles south of Soledad, the Salinas River drops in close to the hillside bank and runs deep and green. The water is warm too, for it has slipped twinkling over the yellow sands in the sunlight before reaching the narrow pool. On one side of the river the golden foothill slopes curve up to the strong and rocky Gabilan mountains, but on the valley side the water is lined with trees – willows fresh and green with every spring, carrying in their lower leaf junctures the debris of the winter's flooding; and sycamores with mottled, white, recumbent limbs and branches that arch over the pool.

💡 *How many adjectives are used in this opening passage? What do you notice about the kinds of adjectives he uses?*

More Writer's Craft

Creating Imagery (cont.)

The following passage uses a simile and a **cliffhanger** (a suspenseful ending) to create an interesting end to the story.

💡 *Can you find the simile and the cliffhanger?*

'Fred,' she shouted, 'that's quite enough – I want to get out of here.' Fred turned round, his dark hair shining in the sunlight like glossy silk. She looked at him and smiled, picked up her bags, walked over to the doorway, went down the path and away…

Finally, look at this key moment from *The Lottery* by Shirley Jackson. The writer uses **repetition**, an adverb, questions and **ellipsis** (…) in this extract. All have been combined to build up the tension.

After that, there was a long pause, a breathless pause, until Mr. Summers, holding his slip of paper in the air, said, 'All right, fellows.' For a minute, no one moved, and then all the slips of paper were opened. Suddenly, all the women began to speak at once, saying, 'Who is it?', 'Who's got it?', 'Is it the Dunbars?', 'Is it the Watsons?' Then the voices began to say, 'It's Hutchinson. It's Bill… Bill Hutchinson's got it.'

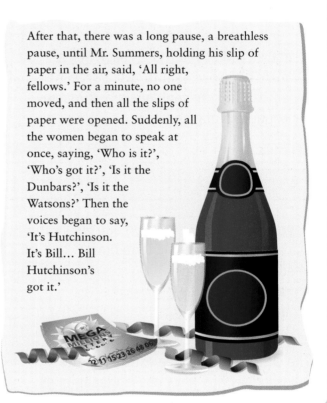

Quick Test

1. What do most adverbs end in?
2. Do adverbs go after the verb or before?
3. What is the effect of using a lot of similar verbs, close together in a text?
4. Why is word order in sentences important?
5. What effect might you achieve by leaving the main subject of a sentence until last?

KEY WORDS
Make sure you understand these words before moving on!
- Verb
- Indicates
- Adverb
- Positioning
- Complex
- Compound
- Cliffhanger
- Repetition
- Ellipsis

Work out the key words from the clues below, then copy and complete the word search.

E	P	H	S	O	H	E	G	U	H	C	L	X	T
N	E	V	L	A	T	M	O	A	Y	L	S	O	P
C	L	T	E	M	I	C	M	D	L	I	P	N	T
R	I	S	C	R	H	E	K	V	D	F	C	V	A
E	P	A	B	D	B	F	S	E	T	F	S	E	S
G	T	B	S	G	A	N	N	R	E	H	S	R	E
N	I	H	Q	I	L	R	G	B	F	A	T	C	P
A	N	I	S	E	T	A	C	I	D	N	I	T	I
H	D	Y	J	P	I	N	H	J	U	G	C	A	L
F	O	A	C	O	M	P	L	E	X	E	N	Z	O
F	N	S	I	S	P	I	L	L	E	R	I	B	N
I	A	D	N	U	O	P	M	O	C	V	N	I	Y
L	P	O	S	I	T	I	O	N	I	N	G	L	Z
C	E	R	E	P	E	T	I	T	I	O	N	K	O

1 A word meaning 'shows'.

2 A series of three dots used to build up suspense or tension.

3 A 'doing' word.

4 A word meaning 'placing'.

5 A type of sentence that has more than one clause, where one clause depends on the other for it to make sense.

6 A word that describes how you do something.

7 A type of sentence that's usually made from a couple of simpler sentences, joined by simpler connectives like 'and' or 'but'.

8 A technique where a word or phrase appears more than once.

9 Ending a story with suspense.

...shows

doing...

placing...

More Writer's Craft

Testing Understanding

1 **Identify the verbs and adverbs in the following passage.**

Ruth ran quickly towards Neil, who dashed nervously out of the way. Cautiously she glanced around, but couldn't see where he'd gone. Breathing deeply, Neil hoped that she wouldn't find him. She'd picked on him in the past, cruelly – and he didn't want her to hurt him again.

2 **Use either verbs or adverbs to make the following passage sound like a quick, exciting event.**

a) Don _____ to the train station _____ . Nicolas, his grandson, was

_____ there, _____ with the car engine revving away. _____ ,

there were no traffic wardens _____ there, so he didn't get _____ for

parking in a restricted area.

b) **Now use different verbs and adverbs to make the passage sound slow and lazy.**

Don _____ to the train station _____ . Nicolas, his grandson, was

_____ there, _____ with the car engine revving away. _____ ,

there were no traffic wardens _____ there, so he didn't get _____ for

parking in a restricted area.

3 **Say whether the following sentences have the main clause...**
- **at the start**
- **at the end**
- **split between the start and the end.**

a) Grant played his guitar badly, because he had a headache.
b) Grant, because he had a headache, played his guitar badly.
c) Mike painted the picture because he was inspired by the weather.
d) Because he was inspired by the weather, Mike painted the picture.
e) Gerald scratched his chin, because it itched.
f) Gerald, because it itched, scratched his chin.

Write a key passage of the middle of a story, using the techniques you have learned in this topic.

The hero of your story discovers something that scares them and they must quickly escape. Build up the tension first and then, after the discovery, create a fast-moving description to describe the feeling of escape.

Step 1: This passage should be made up of three parts, or paragraphs:

a) The build-up of tension.
b) The discovery.
c) The escape.

Jot down your ideas for each section. Where will the passage be set? What will be the discovery? What will your hero have to escape from? Where will he or she escape to?

Step 2: Draft your ideas. Try to use the following techniques:

a) Use sentences with the main clause at the end to build up tension. Use short sentences and questions.
b) Make the discovery short and perhaps use ellipsis.
c) Use lots of fast, active verbs and adverbs to create the feeling of someone rushing to escape.

Step 3: Read your draft out loud. Can you see differences in style, tone and mood between the different parts? If you can't, try adding more of the techniques that you've developed, or change those you've included until you're happy with the overall effect.

Try writing the opening or the ending for the same story. How might you create the 'right' kind of mood using…

- varied sentences?
- verbs and adverbs?

Forms of Persuasion

What is Covered in this Topic?

This topic covers…
- techniques of persuasion
- when and how to use these techniques in a formal or an informal setting.

Persuasive Techniques

Here is a begging letter sent by someone claiming to be down on their luck:

Dear Sir,

A fabulous person like you will surely understand my sad, pitiful predicament. I have no money or family. You must help me. Isn't it only fair that poor, hard-done-to and underprivileged people like me should receive support? Don't we deserve it? Haven't you ever felt like me? In a recent survey, over 95% of people nowadays have financial problems. There must be millions – no billions – of people who are suffering like me. Please, please, please try to understand my difficulties.

Think back to before you started work. You probably had no money. You probably had to rely on others to help you. We've all been in that situation, haven't we?

What if you don't help me? I might starve. I might even die. You wouldn't want that to happen now, would you? Think once – think twice – think help.

What about those people who say that people like me are a drain on society? They simply don't understand how people have suffered. They are cruel, heartless and uncaring. A thoughtful person like you wouldn't want to be considered to be one of them, would you?

Imagine me at Christmas. People will be sitting in their warm, cosy houses, feasting on delicious food and wine, while I will be alone, cold and shivering, picking up the festering scraps at the local bus station, hoping that someone will give me fifty pence to buy a cup of tea.

I'm not asking you to help me because I'm selfish. I'm not asking you to help me because I'm poor. I'm asking you to help me, to save my life.

If you don't, I'll come round your house and steal your telly.

Persuasive Techniques (cont.)

The begging letter on the previous page uses a number of techniques of **persuasion**:

1 **Flattery** – being nice to someone, in the hope that they'll agree to your suggestions.

2 Gaining sympathy / sob stories / **guilt** – make the other person feel sorry for you to get them on your side.

3 **Rhetorical questions** – questions that imply an answer without it being stated.

4 **Statistics** – if you use facts and figures, how can someone disagree?

5 **Repetition** – repeat what you want until the person you're working on gives in. This is used a lot by small children.

6 **Empathy** – putting yourself in the other person's place.

7 **Shock tactics** – scare people into doing what you want.

8 Twisting arguments so that they support your views – this shows that you're thinking of all the views and, therefore, come across as being reasonable.

9 **Emotive** words – often used along with gaining sympathy / sob stories / guilt.

10 Rule of three – three ideas, sequenced so that the final one makes the listener or reader feel as if they're getting a good deal, bargain, or extra value, for example, 'I'm not selling this plate for £10, I'm not selling it for £5, I'm only asking for

£2.50...' It's probably worth 50p, but it sounds as if you're getting a bargain.

11 Threats and **blackmail** – a sinister way of 'persuading' someone.

12 Making deals / **compromise** – meet someone halfway if it means that you'll get most of what you want.

💡 *Can you see these persuasive techniques in the begging letter on page 38?*

Persuading Effectively

To persuade someone effectively, it's not simply a case of using as many techniques as possible.

You need to consider who you're trying to persuade and what you're trying to persuade them to do. You will need to decide whether your persuasion needs to be...
* formal
* informal.

Forms of Persuasion

Techniques of Formal Persuasion

Sometimes you might have to use a more serious and **formal** tone if you're trying to persuade someone in authority, or writing for a serious reason.

For example, you might use a formal tone if you're...

- writing to persuade an authority figure to change their mind about their decision
- writing to persuade a company to give you a refund
- writing to protest about something that you don't like and want changed.

Remember that you need to sound sensible, serious and reasonable.

Can you think of any other situations where you might use a formal tone?

Using Formal Persuasive Techniques

Can you use persuasive techniques in a formal situation? The first two examples are given for you.

1. *Flattery – an experienced, well-respected person of your status...*
2. *Gaining sympathy / sob stories / guilt – the poor, downtrodden pensioners who will suffer from this decision...*
3. *Rhetorical questions*
4. *Statistics*
5. *Repetition*
6. *Empathy*
7. *Shock tactics*
8. *Twisting arguments so that they support your views*
9. *Emotive words*
10. *Rule of three*
11. *Threats and blackmail*
12. *Making deals / compromise*

Why do you think you have to be careful in a formal situation when using...
- *shock tactics?*
- *repetition?*
- *emotive words?*
- *threats?*

Techniques of Informal Persuasion

The situations in which you might want to use **informal** persuasion could include...

- getting a friend to do something they might not want to – for example, go on an outdoor pursuits holiday
- asking your parents for a favour – this might not be written down, but you'll still be using persuasive techniques
- persuading a brother or sister to lend you some money.

The same techniques can be used for informal and formal persuasion.

Using Informal Persuasive Techniques

💡 *Can you use persuasive techniques in an informal situation? The first two examples are given for you.*

1. *Flattery – Debbie... a gorgeous wonderful friend like you would surely lend me that top.*
2. *Gaining sympathy / sob stories / guilt – But Mum, I'll be the only person in my entire class who won't be able to go!*
3. *Rhetorical questions*
4. *Statistics*
5. *Repetition*
6. *Empathy*
7. *Shock tactics*
8. *Twisting arguments so that they support your views*
9. *Emotive words*
10. *Rule of three*
11. *Threats and blackmail*
12. *Making deals / compromise*

💡 *Why might you have to be careful with informal persuasion when using...*

- *flattery?*
- *repetition?*
- *threats and blackmail?*

Quick Test

1. What is flattery?
2. What are emotive words?
3. How do statistics convince someone?
4. What are rhetorical questions?
5. Why is blackmail a risky persuasive technique?

KEY WORDS
Make sure you understand these words before moving on!

- Persuasion
- Formal
- Informal
- Flattery
- Repetition
- Statistics
- Shock tactics
- Emotive
- Blackmail
- Rhetorical questions
- Empathy
- Guilt
- Compromise

Forms of Persuasion

Key Words Exercise

Unscramble the key words in the left-hand column, then match each one with its definition.

UPRAISESON	Questions that only have one implied answer.
LAMFOR	Using complimentary words to someone.
FAILNORM	The technique of getting someone to do what you want.
RATTYELF	Numbers.
LUGIT	Serious and following standards of politeness.
ASQUELCHIERIRONSTOT	What you use when you want to demand someone's attention straight away.
CATSITSSIT	Saying something again and again.
PETITIONER	Not serious – relaxed.
APEMYTH	Technique that involves threatening to reveal bad things about someone, or do bad things to them.
CATCHCOTKISS	Meeting someone halfway.
VIEMOTE	A word that describes the feeling you have when you make someone feel sorry.
LABMALICK	Putting yourself in the other person's place.
CRIMPMOOSE	Descriptive words that tug on the emotions.

Key Words Exercise

Comprehension

Choose the correct options in the following sentences.

1. It's good to start a persuasive letter with *flattery/blackmail/repetition* because it puts the reader in a good mood and gets them on your side. Try to make the reader feel *confused/guilty/happy* so that they want to help you.

2. Be careful if you use *slang/casual description/emotive words* because if you go over the top, your reader will think you're exaggerating and not being serious.

3. A good way to end a persuasive letter is by using some form of *threat/three part repetition/empathy* because it ends on a catchy, punchy, memorable statement.

Testing Understanding

Read the script below, which is an example of informal persuasion.

1. Identify and name the techniques used in the script.

2. What other techniques might the *Little Darling One* have used more successfully?

(Little Darling One is trying to pester a parent to allow him to go to the local Safari Park.)

LD1: Mum?

Mum: Yes dear?

LD1: I think that you're the most intelligent and kind mother a son could wish for. When I see you smile, I feel as I though I've been blessed in having you as my parent. Thank you for being my mother.

Mum: That's very nice dear. Pass me the pork scratching mix would you?

LD1: (Shouting) Mum! YOU'RE NOT LISTENING TO ME! I'M TRYING TO BE NICE – IF YOU DON'T LISTEN TO ME NOW, I'M GOING TO SCREAM!

Mum: Yes, sweetums, mummy is listening. What can I do for you?

LD1: I want to go to the Safari Park. NOW.

Mum: But that's not possible, darling. I can't drive, I'm in the middle of making dinner and, as you can see, I'm looking after next door's cat, making a phone call and writing next week's shopping list.

LD1: It's not fair. Everyone else in the street is allowed to go. I'm the only one in the entire street who's not allowed to. I don't think you love me.

Mum: Of course I do. Perhaps another time, eh?

LD1: That's not good enough. I want to go now. Right now. This instant.

Mum: I don't know...

LD1: Look, I'm not asking you because you pay my pocket money, I'm asking you because I need your permission.

Mum: Well...

LD1: Please please please please please please please please please please. Pretty please. With sugary bits on. If you let me go, I'll even be nice to my sister.

Mum: Oh go on then...

Forms of Persuasion

Skills Practice

Write a letter to your local MP persuading them to help reverse a decision to knock down the local sports centre, as it's the only facility available for young people in the area.

Step 1: Your letter is going to be formal, so look at techniques of formal persuasion and steer clear of techniques that might make you sound unreasonable.

How are you going to start your letter? Flattery is a good technique because it gets the reader on your side. However, in a formal letter you need to be careful that you don't exaggerate and sound false.

Step 2: List the arguments you're going to use, in order. Each idea should be in a separate paragraph, unless you wish to combine some ideas that may be similar.

Decide which persuasive techniques you're going to use for each idea. Finishing your letter using the rule of three technique is a good idea, because it acts as a natural catchy phrase.

Step 3: Read your draft. Do your ideas link together? Have you used connectives at the start of and within paragraphs to show how your ideas are linked?

Step 4: When you've drafted your letter and are happy with how it sounds, ask someone else to read it to see if the tone and style sound reasonable. What may sound fair to you, may not sound fair to someone else, so it's worth getting a second opinion.

Step 5: When you're happy with it, think about how you'll present it. If it's formal, you'll probably want to type it, using a sensible, clear font, or use a good quality pen and your best handwriting. The impression gained from the layout is also part of the persuasive technique.

Extension Activity

To improve your persuasion skills, have a go at writing to a friend to persuade them to go skydiving with you.

Remember you're talking to a friend – that will allow you to be informal.

ESSENTIALS

Year 7
KS3 English
Coursebook Answers

PERSONAL WRITING

Page 6

Quick Test

1. They help you to find information easily.

2. It could be used for bad reasons, e.g. by criminals.

3. It makes you seem more interesting.

4. It makes you sound more reasonable.

5. It saves the reader time in finding out information.

Page 7

Key Words Exercise

1. a

2. b

3. b

4. b

5. c

6. c

Page 9

Testing Understanding

1. **a)** My Top Ten facts; What I Did Today.
   They are explaining things to friends and give reasons why he might not be able to see them etc.
   b) About Me; My Likes; My Top Ten Facts.
   They offer interesting information that people might want to know more about.

2. **a)** 'Anyone who doesn't agree with me is a waste of space'; 'Cuz I'm gonna be famous'.
   b) Someone who uses slang gives the impression that they can't be bothered to use full standard English. They might want to sound cool, etc.

3. **Facts**: My name is Alex.

   If you want my autograph then e-mail me and send me a fiver and then I'll post it to you…

   I like playing the guitar.

   I can't be bothered with school.

   Today I learnt some new chords for the guitar.

   I'll have to sack him.

   Opinions: I'm gonna be famous.

   …they're gonna stop me from getting to the top where I deserve to be.

   I am the best guitar player for my age and anyone who doesn't agree with me is a waste of space.

   …I'm great. I have loads of girls who fancy me and I'm not surprised because, well, who wouldn't?

   I don't need to try hard because I'm gonna be famous.

   The bass player in our band is just rubbish and couldn't play the amazing new song I wrote.

4. **a)** All the layout features and sections are the same, e.g. Name; Personal information; Sections and Headings; Both are written in an informal style and use photos.
   b) Alex's profile uses a background picture. The main photo of Alex is different in style to Robbie's, and the content is quite arrogant.
   c) They reveal Alex's arrogance and self-importance.
   d) Alex gives more opinions than Robbie.
   e) Robbie appears more reasonable. He uses more facts than Alex.

5. Any suitable answer which gives reasons based on your personal opinion and linked to the evidence in the profiles is acceptable. Answers based on the details of the language and content of the profile will be more convincing.

Page 9

Skills Practice & Extension Activity

Please refer to the guide on page 1 of the answer booklet.

SHAKESPEARE

Page 13

Quick Test

1. London.

2. Men and boys.

3. The pit.

4. Shakespeare used the characters' words to describe the scene, rather than by using lighting effects.

Page 14

Key Words Exercise

Gallery –	Raised seats in the theatre
Groundlings –	People who paid a penny to stand and watch a play
Prologue –	An introduction to a play before the main story begins
Bawdy –	Rude and loud
Excavations –	Digs done by archaeologists
Archaeology –	The study of history through digging up the past
Pomp –	Showing-off linked to well-off people
Masque –	A kind of play
Thatch –	Roof material made from straw
Kindled –	Set fire
Syllables –	Beats in a word or a line of text
Syntax –	Changing word order

Anagrams

1. Hamlet
2. Romeo and Juliet
3. Macbeth
4. The Globe
5. Gallery

Page 15

Testing Understanding

1. False
2. True
3. True
4. False
5. False
6. False
7. False
8. True
9. False
10. True
11. True
12. True
13. False
14. False
15. False
16. False
17. True
18. False
19. False
20. True

Page 16

Skills Practice & Extension Activity

Please refer to the guide on page 1 of the answer booklet.

GENRE & SCIENCE FICTION

Page 20

Quick Test

1. No. There are different genres in art, music and film, among others.
2. Science fiction.
3. Yes.

4. No.
5. It gets boring and predictable.

Page 21

Key Words Exercise

Composition –	Something that has been composed or created
Distinctive –	Clear and having definite characteristics
Form –	Shape or structure
Cylinder –	A round, tube-shaped container
Concussion –	The state of being stunned
Cavity –	A hole
Inarticulate –	Not very clearly spoken
Ungovernable –	Not possible to control
Steadfastly –	With determination
Pulsated –	Throbbed
Appendage –	Something added on
Alternative –	A different way of doing something
Technology –	Equipment or machinery designed to do a job
Mage –	A kind of wizard
Dense –	Thick

Page 22

Testing Understanding

1. Style; Composition; Features; Reader; Future technology.
2. Dreamy; Horses and guns.
3. Boring; Use; Original.
4. Style; Appropriate.
5. Adjectives; Similes.

True or False?

1. False
2. True
3. True
4. False
5. False
6. True
7. True
8. True
9. False
10. True

Page 23

Skills Practice & Extension Activity

Please refer to the guide on page 1 of the answer booklet.

THE WRITER'S CRAFT

Page 27

Quick Test

1. Ice; Pancake; Nails.
2. A simile.
3. A metaphor.
4. Alliteration.
5. Words that sound like the thing they are describing, e.g. Moo.
6. Tara was a nervous, trembling child at the dentists.

Page 28

Key Words Exercise

1. Adjective – A word that describes a noun

    Simile – A comparison using 'as' or 'like'

    Metaphor – A comparison where one thing is said to be another

    Clause – A phrase that forms part or all of a sentence

    Alliteration – A group of words close together that begin with the same letter or sound

    Onomatopoeia – A word that sounds like the thing it's describing

    Assonance – Repeated use of similar or identical vowel sounds, in words that are close together

    Personification – A kind of metaphor where abstract or non-human things are given human qualities

    Pathetic fallacy – A kind of metaphor where things from nature are given human qualities

    Abstract – Not real – an idea or concept

Comprehension

1. Adjective
2. Simile
3. Metaphor

Page 29

Testing Understanding

1. Sun smiled: Slowly struggled to succeed in reaching the summit.
2. Rays of the merciless sun.
3. My rucksack felt as heavy as molten lead.
4. The journey was a deadening weight on my mind; I gazed ahead at the towering challenge of the cliff above.
5. Fear and doubt tapped me on the shoulder.
6. The sun smiled; Rays of the merciless sun.
7. Struggled to succeed contains assonance in the repeated 'u'; Roasting, toasting.

Techniques

1. Pathetic fallacy
2. Simile
3. Assonance
4. Alliteration
5. Personification
6. Onomatopoeia
7. Alliteration, assonance and simile
8. Onomatopoeia, alliteration and assonance

Page 30

Skills Practice & Extension Activity

Please refer to the guide on page 1 of the answer booklet.

MORE WRITER'S CRAFT

Page 34

Quick Test

1. 'ly'.
2. They can go before or after the verb.
3. They increase the speed or pace of the text.
4. It determines where the emphasis is placed in the sentence and affects meaning.
5. It can build up tension.

Page 35

Key Words Exercise

1. Indicates
2. Ellipsis
3. Verb
4. Positioning
5. Complex
6. Adverb
7. Compound
8. Repetition
9. Cliffhanger

Page 36

Testing Understanding

1. Verbs – Ran; Dashed; Glanced; See; Breathing; Hoped; Find; Picked; Want; Hurt.

    Adverbs – Quickly; Nervously; Cautiously; Deeply; Cruelly.

2. a)–b) There are many varieties of possible responses. There are no right answers to this.

3. a) Start   d) End
    b) Split   e) Start
    c) Start   f) Split

FORMS OF PERSUASION

Page 41

Quick Test

1. It is being nice to someone in the hope that they will agree to your suggestions.

2. They are words designed to stir up feelings or emotions.

3. They give the impression that an argument is well-researched and, therefore, believable.

4. They are questions that imply a certain answer, without actually giving that answer.

5. It might offend the person it is being used on and have the opposite effect it is intended to.

Page 42

Key Words Exercise

1.
Persuasion –	The technique of getting someone to do what you want.
Formal –	Serious and following standards of politeness.
Informal –	Not serious – relaxed.
Flattery –	Using complimentary words to someone.
Guilt –	A word that describes the feeling you have when you make someone feel sorry.
Rhetorical questions –	Questions that only have one implied answer.
Statistics –	Numbers.
Repetition –	Saying something again and again.
Empathy –	Putting yourself in the other person's place.
Shock tactics –	What you use when you want to demand someone's attention straight away.
Emotive –	Descriptive words that tug on the emotions.
Blackmail –	Technique that involves threatening to reveal bad things about someone, or do bad things to them.
Compromise –	Meeting someone halfway.

Page 43

Comprehension

1. Flattery; Guilty.

2. Emotive words.

3. Three part repetition.

Testing Understanding

1. Flattery; Threats and blackmail; Guilt; Emotive language; Demands; Repetition; Making deals; Rule of three.

2. Rhetorical questions; Statistics; Using all of the same techniques that were used, but more subtly, might have helped too.

PUNCTUATION

Page 48

Quick Test

1. Full stop. 'Donna gets on with everyone. She is a very understanding person.'

2. Hyphen. 'The well-dressed man caught the train.'

3. Colon. 'Dan's favourite saying was often repeated: "Don't do anything that I'd do!"'

4. The Prime Minister's (**possession**) policies didn't (**omission**) please everyone.

5. a) There; Their
   b) Its; It's
   c) Too; To

Page 49

Key Words Exercise

a)	Correct	h)	Incorrect
b)	Incorrect	i)	Correct
c)	Incorrect	j)	Incorrect
d)	Correct	k)	Correct
e)	Correct	l)	Correct
f)	Incorrect	m)	Correct
g)	Incorrect	n)	Correct

Comprehension

1. Punctuation

2. Commas; Full stops

3. Omission; Possession

Page 50

Testing Understanding

The soil below London's streets holds many secrets. It's true to say that people have been living in London for thousands of years, but London has kept many of its secrets – until now. This is one of the secrets: 'An ancient Roman road beneath their garden' was what the headline in the London newspapers said. Mike Fredrickson – who'd lived in Southwark for many years – always wondered what the bits of tile were that he kept digging up and assembling in his shed. After many years of collecting these tiles, Mike and his wife took them to their council office where they heard that there was an archaeologist; an archaeologist who'd tell them what they'd found. Mike's decision to take the bits to the council proved to be inspired. They turned out to be part of a Roman mosaic from a self-contained villa beneath his back garden. Mike's hoping that his discovery will mean that he'll not have to buy a lottery ticket in future.

True or False?

1. False
2. True
3. True
4. False
5. False
6. True
7. False
8. False
9. False
10. True

Page 51

Skills Practice & Extension Activity

Please refer to the guide on page 1 of the answer booklet.

DRAMA TEXTS

Page 55

Quick Test

1. Down Left.
2. Long Shot.
3. Props.
4. For stage directions.
5. To move the camera left or right, up or down.

Page 56

1. Drama
2. Stage directions
3. Properties
4. Brackets
5. Italics
6. Long Shot
7. Medium Shot
8. Close-up
9. Pan
10. Zoom
11. Sound effects
12. Technical
13. Cut
14. Adapted

Page 57

Testing Understanding

1. c
2. b
3. c
4. c
5. a
6. b
7. c

Page 58

Skills Practice & Extension Activity

Please refer to the guide on page 1 of the answer booklet.

READING FOR MEANING

Page 62

Quick Test

1. Skim reading
2. Scanning
3. Extensive reading
4. Intensive reading
5. Fact

Page 63

Key Words Exercise

Comparative – Having put one thing next to another for the process of comparison.

Modal – A word like 'could'.

Conditional – Word that contains or expresses some doubt.

Null comparative – A comparison where you aren't really comparing to anything else.

Disparity – The difference between one thing and another.

Opinions – Things that can't be proved, but which someone believes.

Extensive reading – Reading longer texts.

Origin – Word that means the place where something began.

Personal Voice – One person's view.

Intensive reading – Reading technique where you would study a passage in detail to extract information.

Precipitation – Word meaning 'rainfall'.

Mean – Word which, in this unit, means 'average'.

Scanning – Reading technique designed to identify key facts quickly.

Variations – Word meaning 'differences'.

Skim reading – Reading technique you would use to get a general idea of what something is about.

Fact – Some things that can be proved.

Page 64

Testing Understanding

a) The group called The Credit Card of Hope released their first single on 21st June 2007. It was called *Not Everybody's Got an Angel*.

Their next exposure to the public was on an internet-only radio show where their track received airplay.

At least getting airplay was better than no airplay at all.

All of these songs are kept on a computer hard drive stored in a safe deposit box in Stoke-on-Trent.

Less than 20 MP3s were downloaded…

b) Although it was better than the other tracks on there, in my opinion it didn't get them their much deserved breakthrough and so they had to struggle on.

Finally, it's believed that the group split up in early 2008. A lack of sales probably contributed to this. The group apparently leave behind over 50 songs that the public will never hear.

c) …unluckily failed to make any impression on the charts. They should have made their breakthrough a few months later, when their follow-up track *Everything About You but the Vale* was fortunately included on the cover-mount CD of a football fanzine.

Many listeners found the track *The Jorge Monster Mash* quite funny, even though it wasn't supposed to be.

Page 65

Skills Practice & Extension Activity

Please refer to the guide on page 1 of the answer booklet.

WRITING FOR AN AUDIENCE

Page 69

Quick Test

1. Non-fiction.

2. Generally it should, but opinions in the review might be a little less formal.

3. They give the reader the correct order to follow.

4. They stop the reader from having to take in too much information in one go. They're easier to understand and follow.

5. True.

Page 70

Key Words Exercise

1.	c	5.	a
2.	a	6.	c
3.	b	7.	c
4.	b		

Page 71

Testing Understanding

1.	True	8.	False	15.	False
2.	True	9.	False	16.	True
3.	False	10.	True	17.	False
4.	True	11.	False	18.	True
5.	False	12.	False	19.	True
6.	True	13.	True	20.	False
7.	False	14.	False		

Page 72

Skills Practice & Extension Activity

Please refer to the guide on page 1 of the answer booklet.

WRITING FAIRY TALES

Page 76

Quick Test

1. Features that are traditionally used.

2. True.

3. An idea that has been used too much and has lost most of its effect and become boring.

4. It's a problem that has to be solved by the characters.

5. It's a changed version of something, like a story.

Page 77

Key Words Exercise

Convention –	Typical ways of writing that have developed.
Evolved –	Grown.
Cultures –	Different patterns of behaviour or life, resulting in overall ways of doing things.
Status –	Rank.
Carnivore –	A meat eater.
Third person –	The use of 'he' 'she' or 'it' in sentences.
Genre –	A format or style.
Plot-line –	Basic storyline.
Tradition –	The passing down of some elements of a culture from generation to generation.
Slavish adherence –	Believing something without questioning it.
Traditionalist –	A person who believes in the passed-down ways of doing things.
Adverb –	Words that describe how things are done.
Adaptation –	Different changed versions.
Feature –	Noticeable qualities.
Linear –	In a straight line.
Clichéd –	Repeated so often that it's become boring.
Crisis –	A problem.

Page 78

Testing Understanding

a) Beautiful girl / Princess
Handsome Prince
Set in a wood / forest / castle
Ends 'Happily ever after' or similar
Written in the third person
Uses adverbs
Contains a crisis / problem
Characters make good choices
Characters make bad choices

b) Helpful animals
Helpful magic
Bad magic
Starts with 'Once upon a time'
Giants and / or monsters
Wicked stepmother / witch

Page 79

Skills Practice & Extension Activity

Please refer to the guide on page 1 of the answer booklet.

MEDIA TEXTS

Page 83

Quick Test

1. True.

2. True.

3. False.

4. It's the newspaper name at the top of the front page.

5. It's a story partly written to get people to want to read inside the paper and, therefore, buy the paper.

Page 84

Key Words Exercise

1	a)	Correct	g)	Incorrect
	b)	Incorrect	h)	Incorrect
	c)	Incorrect	i)	Incorrect
	d)	Correct	j)	Correct
	e)	Correct	k)	Incorrect
	f)	Incorrect	l)	Correct

2. Tabloid – A type of newspaper that is smaller in size and contains entertaining as well as serious articles.

Specialist – A word describing magazines aimed at a specific audience.

Local – Based in one region or area.

Teaser – An article on the front of a newspaper which gets the reader to turn the page and read inside.

Masthead – The top of the front page of a newspaper where the name of the paper is.

Facility – A tool on a website which enables you to perform a task or operation.

Blurb – A short piece of text that sums up a book, usually to promote it.

Page 85

Testing Understanding

1.	True	8.	False	15.	False
2.	True	9.	False	16.	True
3.	False	10.	True	17.	True
4.	False	11.	True	18.	True
5.	True	12.	False	19.	False
6.	True	13.	True	20.	True
7.	False	14.	True		

Page 86

Skills Practice & Extension Activity

Please refer to the guide on page 1 of the answer booklet.

ACKNOWLEDGEMENTS

The author and publisher are grateful to the copyright holders for permission to use quoted materials and images.

Every effort has been made to trace copyright holders and obtain their permission for the use of copyright material. The authors and publishers will gladly receive information enabling them to rectify any error or omission in subsequent editions. All facts are correct at time of going to press.

Letts and Lonsdale
4 Grosvenor Place
London SW1X 7DL

School orders: 015395 64910
School enquiries: 015395 65921
Parent and student enquiries: 015395 64913
Email: enquiries@lettsandlonsdale.co.uk
Website: www.lettsandlonsdale.com

ISBN: 978-1905896-653

01/230508

Published by Letts and Lonsdale

© 2008 Lonsdale, a division of Huveaux Plc.

British Library Cataloguing in Publication Data.

A CIP record of this book is available from the British Library.

Book concept and development: Helen Jacobs and Rebecca Skinner

Author: Nicolas Barber
Project Editor: Robert Dean
Cover Design: Angela English
Inside Concept Design: Helen Jacobs and Sarah Duxbury
Text Design and Layout: Jo Hatfield
Artwork: Letts and Lonsdale

Printed and bound in Italy

Letts and Lonsdale make every effort to ensure that all paper used in our books is made from wood pulp obtained from well-managed forests.

Punctuation

What is Covered in this Topic?

This topic looks at...
- common forms of punctuation
- common word errors and confusions.

Common Punctuation

The two most common forms of **punctuation** are the **full stop** and the **comma**. They are also the ones that get mixed up the most.

Full stops are used to separate clauses that each make sense on their own, e.g. Robbie was hungry. He went to buy some food.

Commas are used...
- to separate items in a list, e.g. 'Robbie bought beans, rice and fish for his dinner.'
- before certain connectives, e.g. 'Robbie got indigestion, because of the food he ate for his dinner.'
- after the opening connective or connecting phrase in a sentence, e.g. 'Luckily, Robbie had bought some indigestion tablets.'
- to separate inserted clauses in a sentence, e.g. 'Despite going to the doctor, a man he trusted, Robbie was still feeling ill.'

Adding Commas and Full Stops

The sentence 'Kurt takes photographs it is his hobby' needs a full stop to separate the clauses and make sense. It becomes 'Kurt takes photographs. It is his hobby.' when a full stop is added.

The sentence 'Nick loves to travel he visits the USA at least twice a year' needs a full stop to make complete sense. It becomes 'Nick loves to travel. He visits the USA at least twice a year'.

The sentence 'Phil eats a lot of vegetables although he is allergic to sprouts' needs a comma to separate the clauses, to become 'Phil eats a lot of vegetables, although he is allergic to sprouts'.

The sentence 'Steve lives near to the bakery so he gets bread cheaply' becomes 'Steve lives near to the bakery, so he gets bread cheaply' when a comma is added. It makes more sense when the comma separates the clauses more clearly.

Punctuation

Semi-Colons

Semi-colons are used to...
- separate complicated lists, e.g. 'In the meeting we have Dr. Dave Moreman, Steffs University; Professor Norbert Scragg, Keile University and Mr. Fred Halfbiscuit, University of Palos Park.'
- separate closely-related clauses instead of a full stop, e.g. 'New Mexico is a beautiful place; the land is varied and the people are friendly.'

Colons

Colons are used to...
- introduce an idea, e.g. 'There's one thing you need to know about cabbage: it tastes vile.'
- introduce a list, e.g. 'Jambalaya contains many ingredients: rice, beans, meat and tomatoes.'
- introduce a quotation, e.g. 'The teacher's statement read: It's not what you write; it's how you write it that counts.'

Hyphens and Dashes

A **hyphen** is a mark used to separate two parts of a combined word, e.g. self-obsessed.

A hyphen is used in these examples:
- The award-winning writer thanked the audience.
- The man lacked self-confidence.

A **dash** is a mark used to act like brackets around an inserted clause, e.g. 'My friends – Darren, Debbie and Donna – all like sport.

Apostrophes

There are two kinds of **apostrophe**:

- Apostrophes of **omission** – they replace the missing letters in shortened forms of words, e.g. can't = cannot.
- Apostrophes of **possession** – if a word ends in anything but *s*, add *'s* to show possession, e.g. the girl's book (there is only one girl, so add *'s*).

If a word ends in *s*, place the apostrophe after the *s*, e.g. James' book; the girls' book (there are several girls so put the apostrophe after the *s*).

This rule sometimes causes confusion, because we might write 'James' book', but we might say 'James's book'. Both are acceptable.

Here are some examples where apostrophes of omission are needed:

- Fred wasn't guilty of the crimes he was charged with.
- Too much time on the internet isn't good for you.

Here are some examples where apostrophes of possession are needed:

- Sir's hair was the shortest in class.
- 'Will you help me fix Phillip's bike?' asked Sarah.

There, Their, They're

'**There**', '**their**' and '**they're**' are often confused, especially 'there' and 'their':

- Their – belonging to them, e.g. 'It was their car.'
- There – indicating a place, e.g. 'There is a man over there!'
- They're – shortened version of 'They are', e.g. 'They're coming to see us tonight.'

Here are some examples in using the correct form of 'their', 'there' and 'they're':

- The pupils wanted to do their homework straight away.
- 'They're not paying attention!' moaned the teacher.
- 'Is there a doctor in the house?' shouted the man.
- 'Look over there. They're playing with their new football.'

Punctuation

To, Too and Two

The words 'To', 'Too' and 'Two' are commonly confused.

'To' is used…
- like 'towards', e.g. 'I am going to the shops.'
- with the **infinitive** form of verbs, e.g. 'I am going to run.'

Too means 'also' or 'as well', e.g. 'Are you going? Can I come too?' 'Is it too much?'

Two is the number 2.

Here are some examples of 'to', 'too' and 'two':
- Is it too late?
- Do you want to know who won the lottery?
- You two are too alike to be true!

It's and Its

The use or omission of the apostrophe in 'its' and 'it's' is a common error:
- It's – 'It is' or 'It has', e.g. 'It's going to rain'. 'It's been a long time since I had beans for tea.'
- Its – belonging to 'it', e.g. 'The monkey scratched its chin.' The river burst its banks.'

Here are some examples of 'it's' and 'its':
- The cathedral got its name from the area it was originally built in.
- Whether it's true or not, it still seems strange that aliens would be interested in Earth.
- It's hard to be humble when you're brilliant.

Quick Test

1. Insert a comma or a full stop:
   'Donna gets on with everyone she is a very understanding person.'
2. Add a hyphen or a dash:
   'The well dressed man caught the train.'
3. Add a colon or semi-colon:
   'Dan's favourite saying was often repeated "Don't do anything that I'd do!"'
4. Add apostrophes of omission and possession:
   'The Prime Ministers policies didnt please everyone.'
5. Choose the correct form of each word in the following sentences:
   a) There / their / they're is the man who took there / their / they're money.
   b) The dog was licking it's / its paw. It's / Its a sure sign that it was hurting.
   c) There are to / too / two many people who want to / too / two play football.

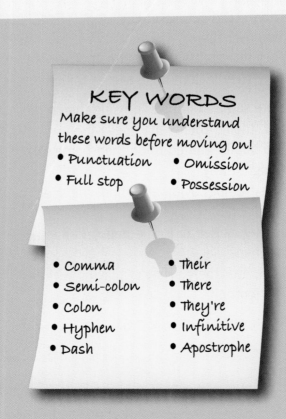

KEY WORDS
Make sure you understand these words before moving on!
- Punctuation
- Full stop
- Omission
- Possession
- Comma
- Semi-colon
- Colon
- Hyphen
- Dash
- Their
- There
- They're
- Infinitive
- Apostrophe

Key Words Exercise

Which key word definitions are correct and which are incorrect?

Keyword	Definition
a) Punctuation	The use of standard marks and signs in writing and printing to separate words into sentences, clauses and phrases in order to clarify meaning.
b) Full stop	A punctuation mark indicating the end of a clause that doesn't make sense on its own.
c) Comma	A punctuation mark indicating the end of a clause that makes sense on its own.
d) Semi-colon	A punctuation mark used to sometimes separate complicated lists.
e) Colon	A punctuation mark used to sometimes introduce a quotation.
f) Hyphen	A punctuation mark used to act like brackets around a clause.
g) Dash	A punctuation mark used to separate two parts of a combined word.
h) Apostrophe	A mark used to show speech.
i) Omission	A word that means 'missed out'.
j) Possession	A word that means 'put an apostrophe after the *s*'.
k) There	A word that indicates direction.
l) Their	A word that means 'belonging to us'.
m) They're	It means 'they are'.
n) Infinitive	The main form of the verb.

Comprehension

1 **Copy and complete the following sentences, using some of the key words above.**

_____ is very important, because your writing will not make sense without it.

2 Be careful that you don't mix up _____ , which separate clauses, and _____ , which separate sentences.

3 Apostrophes of _____ for missed-out letters need to be put in the correct place, as do apostrophes of _____ , which show that something belongs to something else. These are the basic forms of punctuation that people tend to mix up.

Punctuation

Correct the following passage, which has punctuation missing and contains spelling errors.

The soil below Londons streets holds many secrets. Its true to say that people have been living in London for thousands of years but London has kept many of its secrets until now this is one of the secrets 'An ancient Roman road beneath there garden' was what the headline in the London newspapers said. Mike Fredrickson whod lived in Southwark for many years always wondered what the bits of tile were that he kept digging up and assembling in his shed.

After many years of collecting these tiles, Mike and his wife took them to they're council office where they heard that their was an archaeologist an archaeologist whod tell them what theyd found. Mikes decision too take the bits two the council proved to be inspired they turned out to be part of a Roman mosaic from a selfcontained villa beneath his back garden Mikes hoping that his discovery will mean that hell not have two buy a lottery ticket in future.

True or False?

Are the following statements true or false?

1. 'There' means 'belonging to them'.

2. Apostrophes are used for more than one reason.

3. Hyphens and dashes look similar, although they have different uses.

4. It's stands for 'it is', but not 'it has'.

5. Commas can separate sentences.

6. Colons can be used to introduce an idea.

7. Commas separate items in a list, but only the first two.

8. You put an apostrophe on any word ending in *s*.

9. 'To' is the number 2.

10. Commas are used after the opening connective in a sentence.

Skills Practice

Your brief is to create information posters for primary school pupils on the following topics:

- **How to use apostrophes.**
- **Commonly confused words – 'there / they're / there', 'it's / its' and 'to / two / too'.**
- **The differences between commas and full stops.**
- **How to use semi-colons, colons, hyphens and dashes.**

Step 1: Look back over the topic and write your own versions of the rules and definitions you've learned. Simplify the language to make the explanations clearer to younger children.

Step 2: Make up three examples of each rule or definition to go onto each poster. Make sure they're correct.

Step 3: Try to think of catchy ways of remembering the rules. Can you make up any rhymes, pictures or other ways of making people remember the rules that you can put on your posters? Trying to think of ways of remembering the rules is a good way to remember them yourself.

Extension Activity

Design some more posters, but this time choose a different target audience.

a) Adult learners:
- How would you change the text so they didn't feel that you were talking down to them?
- How would you change the font and the pictures on the poster to make it more appealing to them?

b) Your own age group:
- What examples would you choose to make your peers interested?
- How might you use humour to attract their attention?

c) People learning English as a foreign language:
- How would you use images to get round the problem of the readers being new to the language?
- Why might you need a very clear font?

Use the prompts to make sure your posters are appropriate for the audience and get your message across clearly.

Drama Texts

What is Covered in this Topic?

This topic looks at…
- features of drama texts
- differences between types of drama texts.

What is Drama?

Drama is a work of prose or verse, usually telling a story. It's written for actors who play the characters and perform the dialogue and action.

Drama scripts are not just for plays. Films and radio performances use drama scripts too. Each type of script has slightly different features.

The following is an example of a stage script from *The Happy Man*, by H. Adams.

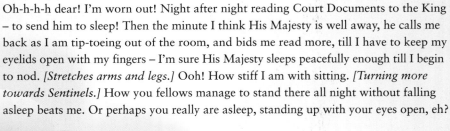

SCENE 1:

[*At the Palace. A Court Room adjoining the King's Bedchamber. Dawn is just about to break. Lights gradually increase as the scene progresses.*]

Two Sentinels on guard, up C.

Chair L. Chair R.

[*Enter the LORD CHAMBERLAIN (L) on tip-toes, carrying a huge book. He is a harassed, fussy little man. He is obviously very tired and flops down on chair (L) dropping the heavy book on the floor, with a loud bang. He jumps up and hisses, Sh------ Sh-------, looking anxiously towards the Royal bedchamber (L). The silent Sentinels remain motionless. The LORD CHAMBERLAIN sits again, gives a terrific yawn and speaks, half to himself and half to the guards, purely for the benefit of the audience.*]

LORD CHAMBERLAIN: Oh-h-h-h dear! I'm worn out! Night after night reading Court Documents to the King – to send him to sleep! Then the minute I think His Majesty is well away, he calls me back as I am tip-toeing out of the room, and bids me read more, till I have to keep my eyelids open with my fingers – I'm sure His Majesty sleeps peacefully enough till I begin to nod. [*Stretches arms and legs.*] Ooh! How stiff I am with sitting. [*Turning more towards Sentinels.*] How you fellows manage to stand there all night without falling asleep beats me. Or perhaps you really are asleep, standing up with your eyes open, eh?

[*No response*]

Features of a Stage Play

A play is set out very differently from a story or poetry and contains different features.

Stage directions are instructions to the actor / actress, which tell them...

- how to move
- where to move
- how to say their lines
- where characters or objects need to be on a stage.

Stage movements are always the same, even if a play is performed in a different theatre. There are standard stage name areas, as seen in the diagram opposite.

💡 *Stage directions are set out differently to speech. Why do you think this is?*
- *In The Happy Man script, where do the two chairs go?*
- *Which side is the Royal bedchamber on?*
- *Where are the two Sentinels standing?*

Properties – props – are the items the actors need for the performance. Sometimes they're printed as a list, or described in the stage directions. It's the Props Manager's job to go through the script and make a list of what's needed.

💡 *Which props are described in The Happy Man and will definitely be needed?*

💡 *Which props are not described, but you think might be needed, because of clues you can work out from the characters and setting?*

Use of **brackets** and **italics** – these are used to separate speech lines from stage directions, so the cast can see the difference between words and actions when learning their lines.

The names of the speakers are at the side of the script to show who is speaking.

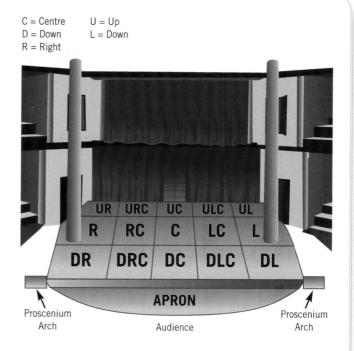

C = Centre   U = Up
D = Down   L = Down
R = Right

UR	URC	UC	ULC	UL
R	RC	C	LC	L
DR	DRC	DC	DLC	DL

APRON

Proscenium Arch

Audience

Proscenium Arch

STAGE PROPS

Drama Texts

Film and Television Scripts

Film and television scripts have similarities with stage play scripts, but there are important differences too.

This example of a television script shows some of the differences in stage directions.

SCENE:	*The inside of a hotel ballroom.*
	[The band have just finished playing and a member of the audience approaches the lead singer]
AUDIENCE MEMBER:	Hi. Would you mind having a word with that girl over there? She doesn't know the difference between Cajun and Zydeco music.
LEAD SINGER:	She doesn't?
AUDIENCE MEMBER:	I'm sure she'd appreciate it if you could go over and explain. She's a bit shy, you see, and doesn't want to ask in person. Her name's Emma.
	[Cut to: Long shot of other band members gazing jealously at the lead singer, who is approaching the girl. They turn to look at each other and nod in agreement]
BAND MEMBER:	Right. That's the final straw. He's got to leave the band now.
	[Cut to close-up of the lead singer and the girl talking]

The writer uses the word '**cut**' in the stage directions. This is for the actors, actresses and **technical crew**, such as the camera and sound operators.

A cut is when the picture quickly changes from one scene to another. Writing a television script is different from writing a stage script because it's for a different audience.

Effects and Shots

Sound effect instructions feature in television and film scripts, although not as much as in a radio script. It might be that the audience are watching a scene and there are different sounds or music on screen at the same time. A television, film or radio scriptwriter has to think of this more than a stage scriptwriter.

There are many types of camera shots:
- LS = **Long Shot** – the camera is looking from a long way away.
- MS = **Medium Shot** – the camera is focused on half of a person's body.
- CU = **Close-up** – the camera goes in close on something or someone.
- **Pan** – the camera moves sideways, or up and down.
- **Zoom** – the camera moves in or out from the subject.

Adapting Texts for Stage and Television

Many successful books are made into films or television programmes. This means that the original novel has to be **adapted** for the screen. Sometimes, parts have to be left out, or new ideas brought in, so that the story works better on screen. This can be seen by comparing the opening of Jane Austen's novel, *Sense and Sensibility*, with its 1995 screenplay.

The novel's opening paragraph has a lot of explanation and little action, so the novel was adapted to make it more exciting for the film version.

> The family of Dashwood had long been settled in Sussex. Their estate was large, and their residence was at Norland Park, in the centre of their property, where, for many generations, they had lived in so respectable a manner as to engage the general good opinion of their surrounding acquaintance. The late owner of this estate was a single man, who lived to a very advanced age, and who for many years of his life, had a constant companion and housekeeper in his sister. But her death, which happened ten years before his own, produced a great alteration in his home; for to supply her loss, he invited and received into his house the family of his nephew Mr. Henry Dashwood, the legal inheritor of the Norland estate, and the person to whom he intended to bequeath it.

The film script goes straight to the important plot events, using stage directions to show what's happening. There are detailed instructions for the camera and technical crew.

 Why might fans of a book not like a film or television version?

EXT. OPEN ROADS – NIGHT – TITLE SEQUENCE

A series of traveling shots. A well-dressed, pompous-looking individual (JOHN DASHWOOD, 35) is making an urgent journey on horseback.
He looks anxious.

EXT. NORLAND PARK – ENGLAND – MARCH 1800 – NIGHT

Silence. Norland Park, a large country house built in the early part of the eighteenth century, lies in the moonlit parkland.

INT. NORLAND PARK – MR DASHWOOD'S BEDROOM – NIGHT

In the dim light shed by candles we see a bed in which a MAN (MR DASHWOOD, 52) lies, his skin waxy, his breathing laboured.

Around him two silhouettes move and murmur, their clothing susurrating in the deathly hush. DOCTORS. A WOMAN (MRS DASHWOOD, 50) sits by his side, holding his hand, her eyes never leaving his face.

MR DASHWOOD (urgent) Is John not yet arrived?

Quick Test

1. On a stage plan, what does 'DL' stand for?
2. In a film script, what does 'LS' stand for?
3. What are 'properties' better known as?
4. What might brackets or italics be used for in a script?
5. In a film script, what does 'pan' mean?

Drama Texts

Key Words Exercise

Work out the key words from the clues below, then find them in the word search.

W	I	B	D	D	E	T	P	A	D	A	S	P	L
L	T	M	R	C	L	O	S	E	U	P	N	Z	O
A	S	E	A	A	H	I	P	O	Z	A	O	E	P
M	C	D	M	C	C	R	E	W	O	N	I	P	S
E	E	I	A	A	B	K	J	K	O	M	T	S	T
T	D	U	E	D	G	L	E	N	M	I	C	K	C
A	R	M	E	F	F	E	F	T	S	Q	E	E	E
L	A	S	D	F	B	R	E	U	S	A	R	T	F
S	M	H	T	A	S	C	I	L	A	T	I	I	F
U	S	O	U	V	E	U	U	C	B	F	D	E	E
D	H	T	O	B	A	T	S	G	D	L	E	S	D
Z	O	W	S	Y	Z	S	T	A	E	O	G	P	N
O	P	T	E	C	H	N	I	C	A	L	A	L	U
O	L	X	T	O	H	S	G	N	O	L	T	A	O
P	R	P	R	O	P	E	R	T	I	E	S	V	S

1 A work of prose or verse that tells a story.

2 They tell actors what to do.

3 Full name for props.

4 They often surround written stage directions.

5 The font style often used for stage directions.

6 When the camera is far away.

7 When the camera is between close and far.

8 When the camera is near.

9 Camera moves sideways or up and down.

10 Camera moves in or out.

11 Noises.

12 The crew who work with cameras and sound.

13 A quick change from one film scene to another.

14 A script that is based on a novel.

Testing Understanding

Complete the following sentences.

1 Drama texts...
   a) are never written in verse
   b) are never written in prose
   c) are mainly written in prose, but sometimes in verse.

2 In the stage direction [Chair L.] the 'L' stands for...
   a) on the left-hand side facing away from the audience
   b) on the left-hand side facing towards the audience
   c) the chair leaning to the left.

3 Stage directions...
   a) tell actors where to stand
   b) tell actors how to say their lines
   c) both a) and b).

4 The word 'Props'...
   a) comes from stands used to support scenery on stage
   b) is a word used in the theatre meaning 'Everything's OK'
   c) is a shortened form of the word 'Properties'.

5 In scripts, speech marks aren't used because...
   a) scripts are nearly all speech anyway
   b) they don't fit on the page
   c) both a) and b).

6 Film and television scripts are different to play scripts because they include...
   a) camera instructions
   b) camera instructions and more sound effects than a stage play
   c) sound effects.

7 In a television or film script, the initials 'CU' stand for...
   a) See You
   b) Camera Up
   c) Close-up.

Drama Texts

Write a drama script for the first scene of a stage play. You can choose the topic, setting and plot.

Step 1: Decide where your play is set, what's going to happen and how many characters will be involved. Don't forget to include characters that appear on stage but don't speak. Make a list so that you remember who to include.

Step 2: Start by writing a stage direction describing the opening scene on the stage. Use the correct way of describing positions of furniture, props and actors/actresses.

Step 3: Begin writing your lines. If you want characters to say things in a certain way, remember to include stage directions for the actors, which give help and advice about this.

When writing speech, remember to think about how speech differs from normal prose. You might include pauses, repetition, stuttering and slang if the characters require it.

Step 4: Complete the draft of your script and read it through with a friend – does it sound the way it should? Are your stage directions clear? Can other people work out from your script how they should stand and move? If anything needs to be changed, redraft it before you complete the final version.

If you want to perform your play, make a copy of the script for every person who needs one, including each actor or actress, and the director if there is one.

Extension Activity

Adapt your play script into a television script.

Alternatively, write a television script from scratch on a new subject. You could also try adapting a favourite story into a television or film script.

Reading for Meaning

What is Covered in this Topic?

This topic looks at…
- different reading styles
- how to create a factual account
- spotting the differences between facts and opinions.

Reading Techniques

There are different ways to read texts. It depends on…
- what kind of text it is
- why we need to read it.

These are the main reading techniques:
- **Skim reading** – running your eyes over the text. You don't take everything in – you just get a general idea of what it's about.
- **Scanning** – reading quickly in order to find specific pieces of information.
- **Extensive reading** – reading to obtain a general understanding of a subject and reading longer texts for pleasure.
- **Intensive reading** – reading shorter texts to find specific information.

For example, you would use different reading techniques for the following situations:
- Skim reading to get an idea of the main news of the day from a newspaper.
- Intensive reading of a section of a contract.
- Scanning the TV section of a newspaper to see what time a programme is on.
- Extensive reading of a novel before you go to bed each night.
- Intensive reading of a travel brochure to find information on a particular hotel.
- Scanning a magazine to see which articles you'd like to read in more detail later.

Reading for Meaning

Using Reading Techniques

When you're scanning for information, you need to keep in mind the key words that apply to what you're looking for. You should look for other versions of those key words, or words with similar meaning.

The following passage contains a lot of detail about the weather in the Lake District, some of which may be relevant to a walker. To find out certain facts or information, a walker may quickly scan it to pick out the details and the key words that are important to their journey.

Scan the passage to find out when the driest and warmest times to visit the Lake District would be. Keep in mind relevant key words like 'dry' and 'warm'.

The Lake District is on the northwest coast of England. Its location and its mountains make it the dampest, wettest part of England. The UK Met Office reports average annual precipitation of more than 2,000 millimetres (80in), but with quite large local variations. The entire area has above average rainfall, but there's a wide disparity between the amount of rainfall in the eastern and western lakes. The rainfall is caused by the mountains.

Seathwaite in Borrowdale is the wettest inhabited place in the British Isles, with average rainfall of 3,300 millimetres (130in) a year. Nearby, Sprinkling Tarn is even wetter than this, recording over 5,000 millimetres (200in) per year. In contrast, Keswick, at the end of Borrowdale, receives 1,470 millimetres (60in) per year, and Penrith (just outside the Lake District) only 870 millimetres (30in). The driest months are usually March to June, with October to January the wettest. However, at lower ground levels there is little difference between months.

The Lake District is a windy place, although sheltered valleys experience gales on average only five days a year. The coastal areas have 20 days of gales and the mountain tops can have 100 days of gales per year.

The sea climate means that the Lake District has relatively moderate temperature variations through the year. Mean temperature in the valleys ranges from about 3°C (37°F) in January to 15°C (59°F) in July. (Moscow, in comparison, at the same latitude, ranges from -10°C to 19°C / 14°F to 66°F)

Snow is expected during winter but the low height of many hills means that they can be snow-free at any time of the year. Normally, significant snowfall only occurs between November and April. On average, snow falls on the mountain, Helvellyn, 67 days per year. During the year, valleys typically experience 20 days of snow falling, a further 200 wet days, and 145 dry days.

When reading intensively, you need to go backwards and forwards over the text to sort out the information that you need.

Read the passage more closely to find...
- *the best parts of the Lake District to visit for weather and the best times to go*
- *the worst parts of the Lake District to visit for weather and the worst times to go.*

Facts and Opinions

It's important to be able to tell the difference between **fact** and **opinion**. For example, if you wanted to find a good hotel, you'd want to know what facilities it offered but also what other people thought of it.

The brochure for the hotel might contain a mixture of facts and opinions. While you would probably accept the facts as true, you would want to check the opinions carefully.

The following passage is an example of the difference between fact and opinion. The facts are highlighted in red and the opinions are highlighted in blue.

Robin Hood, it is believed, was a famous outlaw, who apparently lived in Sherwood Forest. His main rival was alleged to be the Sheriff of Nottingham and his wife was supposed to be Maid Marian. These details are what we think we know from famous legend, but the truth may be somewhat different.

The Court records for York mention a 'Robert Hude' who was seen before the court in 1226. In 1227, the same man was referred to as 'Robinhud'. In 1226, it is also recorded that the Sheriff of Nottingham, a man named William De Grey, was in conflict with a group of outlaws in Sherwood Forest, according to contemporary documents – 1266, 40 years later. It could be that a number of people built upon the legend of the outlaw and over time, the legend grew.

In the grounds of Kirklees Priory, there is a grave marker with the name 'Robard Hude'. Is this proof that the story was true? It would be nice to think so.

The facts in the passage above are identified by the following:

- They contain numbers, e.g. dates and figures.
- The verbs in the sentences are strong and express clear, definite ideas.
- They contain names that can be checked.
- They refer to the **origin** of their information.

Can you see how the facts in the passage above can be identified in these ways?

Opinions are identified by the following:

- They contain **conditional** words or phrases, e.g. 'supposedly'.
- They use **modals**, e.g. 'would', 'could', 'might'.
- **Personal voice** is used and/or opinions are given, e.g. 'I think.'

Can you see how the opinions in the passage above can be identified in these ways?

Reading for Meaning

Opinions as Facts

Skilful writers can give opinions that sound like facts, which you have to be careful of when reading. Look at the following statements:

- Fact – The Battle of Hastings took place in 1066.
- Opinion presented as fact – The gruesome Battle of Hastings took place in 1066.

Adding one word to the sentence has changed the fact into opinion. Who is to say that the Battle of Hastings was 'gruesome'? By adding an adjective which suggests a judgement is being made, the fact has been changed into an opinion.

If you add a **comparative** adjective to a sentence, it can still stay as a fact. For example...

- the Empire State building is *taller* than the Eiffel Tower
- Luke is the *smallest* boy in the class.

In both examples the adjectives are used to compare two or more things.

If you use a **null comparative**, however, the sentence becomes an opinion, because you're not comparing it properly to another thing.

For example...

- our burgers are better
- Robert is taller.

Here are some examples of facts:

- World War Two lasted from 1939 to 1945.
- 36 people caught the Hanley bus today.

Here are some examples of opinions presented as facts:

- 2 unlucky people were involved in an accident.
- In 1066, King Harold was unluckily defeated at the Battle of Hastings.

Quick Test

1. What kind of reading is used when you quickly run your eyes over a text?
2. What kind of reading is used when you quickly find specific information?
3. What is reading for pleasure classed as?
4. What is reading shorter texts in order to extract specific information called?
5. Is this statement a fact or an opinion presented as fact? 'The girls were smaller than their brothers.'

Key Words Exercise

Match each key word with its definition.

Comparative	A comparison where you aren't really comparing to anything else.
Modal	Word meaning 'rainfall'.
Conditional	Reading technique designed to identify key facts quickly.
Null comparative	Word that means 'the place where something began'.
Disparity	One person's view.
Opinions	Some things that can be proved.
Extensive reading	Word that contains or expresses some doubt.
Origin	Reading technique where you would study a passage in detail to extract information.
Personal voice	Word which, in this topic, means 'average'.
Intensive reading	Things that can't be proved, but which someone believes.
Precipitation	A word like 'could'.
Mean	Reading technique you would use to get a general idea of what something is about.
Scanning	Word meaning 'differences'.
Variations	The difference between one thing and another.
Skim reading	Reading longer texts.
Facts	Having put one thing next to another for the process of comparison.

Reading for Meaning

Testing Understanding

Skim read the following passage to get a general idea of what it's about. Then scan it to identify...

a) all the facts

b) all the opinions

c) all the opinions pretending to be facts.

Finally, read it intensively to make sure that what you've found is correct.

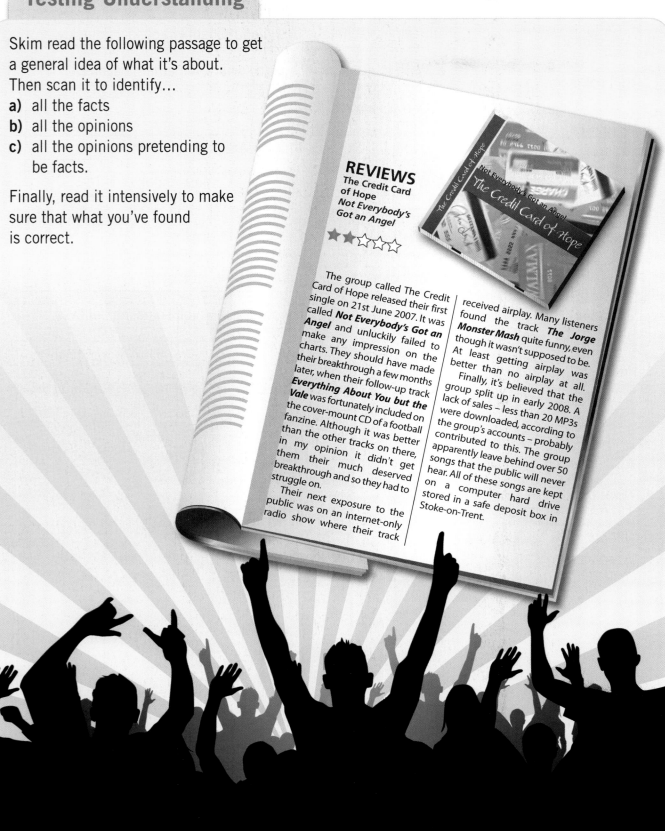

REVIEWS
The Credit Card
of Hope
Not Everybody's
Got an Angel

★★☆☆☆

The group called The Credit Card of Hope released their first single on 21st June 2007. It was called **Not Everybody's Got an Angel** and unluckily failed to make any impression on the charts. They should have made their breakthrough a few months later, when their follow-up track **Everything About You but the Vale** was fortunately included on the cover-mount CD of a football fanzine. Although it was better than the other tracks on there, in my opinion it didn't get them their much deserved breakthrough and so they had to struggle on.

Their next exposure to the public was on an internet-only radio show where their track received airplay. Many listeners found the track **The Jorge Monster Mash** quite funny, even though it wasn't supposed to be. At least getting airplay was better than no airplay at all.

Finally, it's believed that the group split up in early 2008. A lack of sales – less than 20 MP3s were downloaded, according to the group's accounts – probably contributed to this. The group apparently leave behind over 50 songs that the public will never hear. All of these songs are kept on a computer hard drive stored in a safe deposit box in Stoke-on-Trent.

Skills Practice

Write a passage about a hotel for a travel brochure. Make the hotel sound a reasonable place to stay, without telling lies. Include a mixture of...

- **facts**
- **opinions**
- **opinions presented as facts.**

Step 1: Here are the available facts about the place you're going to write about. Decide which of the following facts to group together as paragraphs:

Hotel Sunny Vista	75 rooms – all doubles
5 minutes from the beach – by car	38 rooms have a sea view
Hotel is next door to the sewage works	All rooms have ensuite facilities
25 rooms have a balcony, facing the sewage works	The hotel was voted 'Best Hotel in Town' in 2002 – before the sewage works were built
The average temperature in August, recorded outside the hotel, was 35°C	The hotel is facing a 24-hour supermarket

Step 2: Some of the facts about the hotel make it sound good. How might you change them, using opinions presented as facts, to make the hotel sound better?

Example – People believed, in 2002, that the hotel was the best in town and this might still be the case now.

How might you phrase the 'bad' things to make them sound better? Try using personal opinions for this.

Step 3: When you've drafted your description, give it to someone else to read and ask them if it would be the kind of hotel they would stay at. Ask them if they have any doubts about the way the hotel is described. If they have doubts, look at those parts of your description and see if you can make them sound more factual and convincing.

Extension Activity

In a brochure, photos would accompany the descriptions. Have a look at some travel brochure photographs.

Why do you think that brochures tend to have lots of close-up shots of hotels and not many photos that show the hotel's surroundings?

How does this clever framing of photographs act like the photographer's opinion?

Writing for an Audience

What is Covered in this Topic?

This topic covers...
- how to use features of non-fiction writing
- how to write for a real audience.

Writing Letters

If a new MP3 player was already broken when it was delivered and was bought at a shop miles away, you could write a letter asking for a refund or a replacement.

The temptation with faulty goods is to get angry and demand your money back. That's probably not a good idea at first, as it may upset or annoy the person who you bought it from. They may feel offended by the words you use. Then you might not get your money back, or a replacement, as quickly as you would like.

In the letter you would need to include...
- the date
- what you bought
- when you bought it – details of **receipts**, etc.
- what's wrong with it
- what you would like to happen
- your contact information.

Using a formal style will show that you're business-like and **efficient**, as will making sure there are no mistakes or crossings-out.

Customer Services

Letters of Complaint

Here's a letter of complaint that was sent about a similar problem. It's not a good example of how to complain!

💡 *What do you think is wrong with this letter?*

Dear Mr. Manager,

I can't believe the ~~rubbish~~ rubbish you sell in your shop. Only the other day, I bought this new MP3 player and it was smashed to bits when I took it out of the box at home! You want to watch what you sell, you do, or you could get in trouble.

Anyway, I want my money back or there's going to be big trouble. My uncle works for the police and he'll come round your shop and arrest you if you don't sort this out immediately. If I haven't heard from you within 4 days of you ~~getting~~ getting this letter, then I'll see you in court.

I'm also going to tell all my friends how bad your shop is. Fancy selling broken rubbish like this and charging good money for it! Unbelievable!

If you want this broken MP3 player back, you'll have to let me know, but you'll have to pay for the postage.

Yours truly,

Gerald Dowd

Adding Important Information

Try to learn from the mistakes made above when you draft your own letter:

- Use the name of a person when you're writing to them, if you know it. It will help to direct your complaint to the person who will deal with it more quickly. It also means that you're able to adopt a more personal, reasonable tone.
- Put a date on your letter. This helps you and the company you are writing to track the progress of the complaint.
- Put your contact details on the letter. If you don't, they won't be able to contact you.

Writing for an Audience

Reviews

Reviews are a form of **non-fiction** writing.

Reading product reviews before buying something can warn you if the item is fragile or easily breakable.

Below is a review of the MP3 player that was complained about.

💡 *Which of the following features does the review share with the complaint letter? Which are different features?*
- *Formal style.*
- *Use of specialist vocabulary.*
- *Well-presented layout.*
- *Use of headings.*
- *Name of the writer included.*
- *Use of personal opinion.*

May 2008

GO GADG

200+ GIFT IDEAS INSIDE

gadg
musi
plus mu

NEW MP3 PLAYER FAILS TO DELIVER

RATINGS: ★☆☆☆☆

There were high expectations from this latest version of Zipple's ground-breaking MP3 player, but, unfortunately, those expectations have been dashed. On paper, the Zipple Classic offers incredible **specification** – a 320 gig hard drive, **compatibility** with 12 different music formats including *.flac and *.ogg files, the ability to play back and record video, connectors for 3 types of headphones and a composite and HDMI TV connection. Unfortunately, it's a case of a "quart in a pint pot". The playback on all formats is subject to incredible delays as the processor is simply too weak to cope with the demands placed on it.

The size and positioning of the audio and video connectors is also very confusing. Instead of placing video on one side and audio on the other, the two are mixed and as a result it's all too easy to plug the wrong lead into the wrong socket, with **potentially** expensive damage resulting.

Assuming that you've got good eyesight to find the right connections and you're happy to wait 30 seconds for each media file to play, the sound quality is exceptional – until the machine starts to stutter and the playback is interrupted.

No doubt there will be a number of early **adopters** of technology who will rush out and buy this, but a more sensible option would be to wait for the design and software bugs to be sorted out and buy version 2, which must surely follow later this year. Disappointing.

Review by Scott Ligon

Instructions

Instructional writing is very important. If instructions are written well, they make an item easier to operate and make sure that the item is used correctly. If they're poorly written, then things could go wrong.

Below is a set of basic instructions for the Zipple Classic MP3 player.

The instructions are written as a numbered list to allow the reader to follow them in the correct order.

Diagrams are used to help clear up things that aren't obvious just from the words.

Short, simple sentences help the reader take things one step at a time. The word 'you' is used frequently to talk directly to the reader, who is following the instructions.

Formal vocabulary is used so that instructions can be understood by as wide a range of people as possible.

Brackets are used to add extra detail to the main advice and instructions.

Imperative verbs are used to tell someone directly – often near to or at the start of an instruction – what they should do.

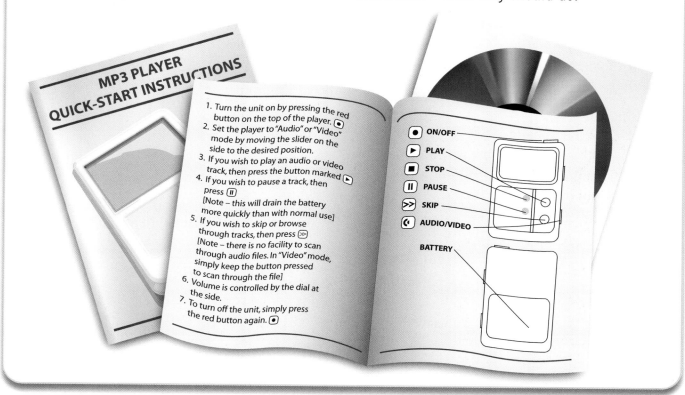

MP3 PLAYER QUICK-START INSTRUCTIONS

1. Turn the unit on by pressing the red button on the top of the player. ⦿
2. Set the player to "Audio" or "Video" mode by moving the slider on the side to the desired position.
3. If you wish to play an audio or video track, then press the button marked ▶
4. If you wish to pause a track, then press (❚❚)
   [Note – this will drain the battery more quickly than with normal use]
5. If you wish to skip or browse through tracks, then press ⊠
   [Note – there is no facility to scan through audio files. In "Video" mode, simply keep the button pressed to scan through the file]
6. Volume is controlled by the dial at the side.
7. To turn off the unit, simply press the red button again. ⦿

⦿ ON/OFF
▶ PLAY
■ STOP
❚❚ PAUSE
⊠ SKIP
◖ AUDIO/VIDEO

BATTERY

Quick Test

1. Is a letter of complaint an example of fiction or non-fiction?
2. Should a review always have a formal style?
3. Why are numbered lists good for instructions?
4. Why are short sentences good in instructions?
5. Brackets are used to add extra information to instructions – true or false?

Writing for an Audience

Key Words Exercise

What is the correct definition of each key word?

1 Non-fiction
a) Stories
b) Scientific documents
c) Prose writing that is not made up

2 Receipt
a) A written acknowledgment of having received a specified amount of money, goods, etc.
b) A piece of paper
c) Something you throw away

3 Efficient
a) Useful and helpful
b) Performing in the best way possible, combining maximum output with the least effort
c) Well-behaved

4 Specifications
a) A list
b) A detailed set of requirements or features
c) The order in which things work

5 Compatibility
a) Capable of being used with something else
b) Able to be like something else
c) A useful list

6 Potentially
a) Definitely
b) Certainly
c) Possibly

7 Adopters
a) People who do things wrong
b) People who won't try new things
c) People who take on new things

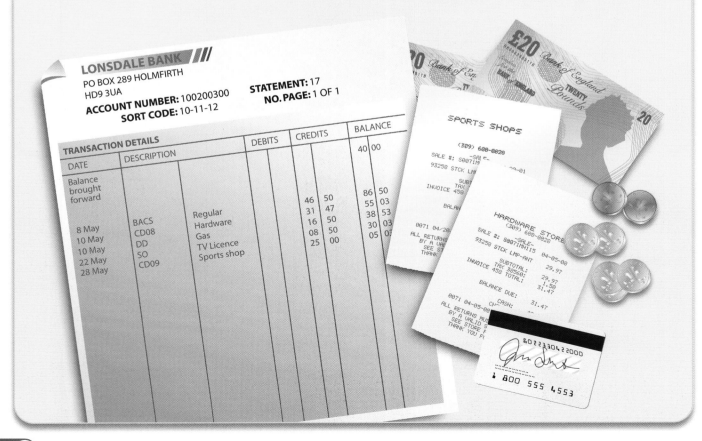

Testing Understanding

Are the following statements about non-fiction writing true or false?

1. In a letter of complaint you should include the date you sent the letter.

2. In a letter of complaint you should use a formal tone.

3. In a letter of complaint it's good to be sarcastic.

4. In a letter of complaint you should say to the person you are complaining to what you want them to do.

5. You don't need to include your contact information in a complaint letter, as the person you're writing to should have it.

6. In a letter of complaint you should use the name of the person that you're writing to, if possible.

7. It doesn't matter about the layout of a complaint letter.

8. In a review, you should always include a picture.

9. In a review, you shouldn't use specialist language.

10. In a review it's normal to include the name of the person writing the review.

11. In a review you shouldn't include opinions.

12. In a review you shouldn't include facts.

13. Headings are helpful when writing a review.

14. Instructions don't need to be in any particular order.

15. Instructions should mainly use complex, lengthy sentences.

16. Diagrams help people to understand instructions.

17. Brackets are used for instructions that the writer has forgotten to include.

18. Instructions should mainly use formal vocabulary.

19. Instructions might speak directly to the person using them.

20. Non-fiction writing can include stories.

Writing for an Audience

Write a review of a brand new wrist watch, the Tick-Tock 1200Z, giving your opinions on it.

The review must be between 200 and 250 words and mention the following features of the watch:

- It has a stopwatch and lap-counter.
- It's solar powered so will never need a new battery.
- It's voice-controlled.
- It has a large, clear display.
- It's available in men's and women's designs.
- It's made from shock- and water-proof materials.
- It's very expensive compared to similar watches.

Step 1: Think of a heading for your review that quickly tells the reader your overall opinion of the watch. Decide what order you're going to put your ideas in – make a paragraph-by-paragraph list.

Step 2: Draft your ideas and count how many words you've written. Keep within the word limit, because you're writing for a magazine that only has a certain amount of space. To save space, take out repeated phrases, combine sentences and ideas and decide which information is essential.

Step 3: Choose a rating for your review that matches the overall opinion you've given. Find a review of a similar product in a magazine and look at how much space you will have to write it up. Write your final draft to fit that same space.

Step 4: Find and add an appropriate picture to go with the review. Use ideas from the layout and vocabulary of actual articles to make your writing seem authentic and realistic.

Extension Activity

Imagine that you've bought the watch, but after a few weeks it stops working. Write a letter of complaint asking for a refund or a replacement.

Writing Fairy Tales

What is Covered in this Topic?

This topic looks at...
- how to write to entertain
- how to use conventions of the fairy tale genre.

Features of Fairy Tales

Most people experience fairy tales at some time, either by having them read to us, reading them ourselves, or watching film **adaptations**.

Fairy tales have **evolved** over time so we don't know who wrote many of them – even the Brothers Grimm and Hans Christian Andersen developed their versions from earlier tales that had been passed down.

Nowadays, new versions of fairy tales are created, which use the **conventions** of these earlier stories – films such as *Shrek* or *Enchanted* are two good examples of this.

These stories share many common **features**, such as...
- characters
- ideas
- **plot-lines**.

People may give different examples and features of the same story because they are different versions of the same fairy tale. There's no 'right' version – just a different way of telling the story.

💡 *Can you think of any fairy tales that contain the following features?*
- *Fairy godmothers.*
- *Wicked stepmothers.*
- *Handsome Princes.*
- *Animals coming to life.*
- *Woods and forests.*
- *A princess – or a beautiful but hard-done-to young woman.*
- *Giants and monsters.*
- *Spells and curses.*
- *Happy endings.*

Writing Fairy Tales

Different Versions

There are many different versions of fairy tales. For example, the story of Cinderella has different versions that come from different **cultures** and **traditions**.

The following extract is from a Scottish version called *Rashin-Coatie*.

💡 *What typical fairy tale features can you see in this passage?*
- *What types of characters are there?*
- *How is the story typical?*
- *How is the language typical?*

Rashin Coatie

Once, a long time ago, there was a gentleman had two lassies. The oldest was ugly and ill natured, but the youngest was a bonnie lassie and good; but the ugly one was the favourite with her father and mother. So they ill-used the youngest in every way, and they sent her into the woods to herd cattle, and all the food she got was a little porridge and whey.

Well, amongst the cattle was a red calf, and one day it said to the lassie, 'Gee that porridge and whey to the doggie, and come wi' me.'

So the lassie followed the calf through the wood, and they came to a bonnie hoosie, where there was a nice dinner ready for them; and after they had feasted on everything nice they went back to the herding.

Every day the calf took the lassie away, and feasted her on dainties; and every day she grew bonnier. This disappointed the father and mother and the ugly sister. They expected that the rough usage she was getting would take away her beauty; and they watched and watched until they saw the calf take the lassie away to the feast. So they resolved to kill the calf; and not only that, but the lassie was to be compelled to kill him with an axe. Her ugly sister was to hold his head, and the lassie who loved him had to give the blow and kill him.

She could do nothing but greet [weep]; but the calf told her not to greet, but to do as he bade her; and his plan was that instead of coming down on his head she was to come down on the lassie's head who was holding him, and then she was to jump on his back and they would run off. Well, the day came for the calf to be killed, and everything was ready – the ugly lassie holding his head, and the bonnie lassie armed with the axe. So she raised the axe, and came down on the ugly sister's head; and in the confusion that took place she got on the calf's back and they ran away. And they ran and better nor ran till they came to a meadow where grew a great lot of rashes; and, as the lassie had not on many clothes, they pu'ed rashes, and made a coatie for her. And they set off again and travelled, and travelled, till they came to the king's house. They went in, and asked if they wanted a servant. The mistress said she wanted a kitchen lassie, and she would take Rashin-Coatie…

Alternative Fairy Tales

Some fairy tales make fun of the genre, as seen in the following version of *Little Red Riding Hood* by James Finn Garner.

There once was a young person named Red Riding Hood who lived with her mother on the edge of a large wood. One day her mother asked her to take a basket of fresh fruit and mineral water to her grandmother's house – not because this was womyn's work, mind you, but because the deed was generous and helped engender a feeling of community. Furthermore, her grandmother was not sick, but rather was in full physical and mental health and was fully capable of taking care of herself as a mature adult...

...On the way to Grandma's house, Red Riding Hood was accosted by a wolf, who asked her what was in her basket. She replied, 'Some healthful snacks for my grandmother, who is certainly capable of taking care of herself as a mature adult.'

The wolf said, 'You know, my dear, it isn't safe for a little girl to walk through these woods alone.'

Red Riding Hood said, 'I find your sexist remark offensive in the extreme, but I will ignore it because of your traditional status as an outcast from society, the stress of which has caused you to develop your own, entirely valid, worldview. Now, if you'll excuse me, I must be on my way.'

Red Riding Hood walked on along the main path. But, because his status outside society had freed him from slavish adherence to linear, Western-style thought, the wolf knew a quicker route to Grandma's house. He burst into the house and ate Grandma, an entirely valid course of action for a carnivore such as himself. Then, unhampered by rigid, traditionalist notions of what was masculine or feminine, he put on Grandma's nightclothes and crawled into bed.

Although the writer is having fun with the features of the genre, he is still using those same features. The story has been changed to make it less offensive and politically-correct, and this has made it funnier.

- *How has the story been changed to make it less offensive?*

- *What fairy tale features can you see in this version?*

Writing Fairy Tales

Creating Your Own Fairy Tale

Fairy tales can be changed in many ways to entertain the reader.

A fairy tale could be created by picking one feature from each category below to create the outline for an original story. You might come up with a strange story to fit these features together, but it would be recognisable as a fairy story because it would contain traditional features.

Good Male Character
Prince Charming, Jack, Buttons, Aladdin, Any random handsome prince!, Dick Whittington

Good Female Character
Snow White, Cinderella, Rapunzel, Sleeping Beauty, Red Riding Hood, Princess Jasmine

Evil Character
Wicked witch, Wicked stepmother, Ugly sisters, Magic talking mirror, Old woman, Sheriff of Nottingham

Random other Character
Woodcutter, Cute animal(s), Dwarf, Cat, Wizard, Dragon

Magic
3 wishes, Kiss, Poisoned apple, Magic Word, Lamp, Magic Beans

Setting
Cottage, Wood / Forest, Castle, Garden, Dungeon, Cave

Common Features

Fairy tales can also use several other common styles and features:

- They often use **clichéd** phrases, beginning with 'Once upon a time' and ending with 'Happily ever after'.
- They're often written in the **third person**.
- They contain sentences that begin with, or use, **adverbs**, e.g. 'Suddenly, Cinderella noticed that it was nearly midnight…'
- There will be a problem at the start of the story – a **crisis** – which will be solved after many trials.
- Good people end up happy and bad people end up unhappy.
- Characters make good and bad choices, but they learn from them to become better people.

💡 *How true are these features of the fairy tales that you know?*

Quick Test

1. What are conventions?
2. There are different versions of most fairy tales – true or false?
3. What is a cliché?
4. What is meant by a 'crisis' in fairy tales?
5. What is an adaptation?

KEY WORDS
Make sure you understand these words before moving on!
- Plot-line
- Linear
- Genre
- Evolved
- Feature
- Clichéd
- Culture
- Tradition
- Adverb
- Status
- Adaptation
- Carnivore
- Traditionalist
- Slavish adherence
- Convention
- Crisis
- Third person

Key Words Exercise

Match each key word with its definition.

Key Word	Definition
Convention	Different patterns of behaviour or life, resulting in overall ways of doing things.
Evolved	Basic storyline.
Cultures	A problem.
Status	The passing down of some elements of a culture from generation to generation.
Carnivore	Believing something without questioning it.
Third person	A meat eater.
Genre	Typical ways of writing that have developed.
Plot-line	A format or style.
Tradition	A person who believes in the passed-down ways of doing things.
Slavish adherence	Different changed versions.
Traditionalist	Noticeable qualities.
Adverb	Grown.
Adaptation	The use of 'he' 'she' or 'it' in sentences.
Feature	Words that describe how things are done.
Linear	Rank.
Clichéd	Repeated so often that it's become boring.
Crisis	In a straight line.

Writing Fairy Tales

Read the following fairy tale, *The Real Princess*, by Hans Christian Andersen.

There was once a Prince who wished to marry a Princess; but then she must be a real Princess. He travelled all over the world in hopes of finding such a lady; but there was always something wrong. Princesses he found in plenty; but whether they were real Princesses it was impossible for him to decide, for now one thing, now another, seemed to him not quite right about the ladies. At last he returned to his palace quite cast down, because he wished so much to have a real Princess for his wife.

One evening a fearful tempest arose, it thundered and lightened, and the rain poured down from the sky in torrents: besides, it was as dark as pitch. All at once there was heard a violent knocking at the door, and the old King, the Prince's father, went out himself to open it.

It was a Princess who was standing outside the door. What with the rain and the wind, she was in a sad condition; the water trickled down from her hair, and her clothes clung to her body. She said she was a real Princess.

'Ah! We shall soon see that!' thought the old Queen-mother; however, she said not a word of what she was going to do; but went quietly into the bedroom, took all the bed-clothes off the bed, and put three little peas on the bedstead. She then laid twenty mattresses one upon another over the three peas, and put twenty feather beds over the mattresses. Upon this bed the Princess was to pass the night.

The next morning she was asked how she had slept. 'Oh, very badly indeed!' she replied. 'I have scarcely closed my eyes the whole night through. I do not know what was in my bed, but I had something hard under me, and am all over black and blue. It has hurt me so much!'

Now it was plain that the lady must be a real Princess, since she had been able to feel the three little peas through the twenty mattresses and twenty feather beds. None but a real Princess could have had such a delicate sense of feeling.

The Prince accordingly made her his wife; being now convinced that he had found a real Princess. The three peas were however put into the cabinet of curiosities, where they are still to be seen, provided they are not lost.

Wasn't this a lady of real delicacy?

Look at the table below.

a) **Identify all the features that appear in the story of *The Real Princess*.**

b) **Which features are not present?**

Beautiful girl / Princess	Handsome Prince	Helpful animals	Set in a wood / forest / castle	Helpful magic
Contains a crisis / problem	Characters make bad choices	Wicked stepmother / witch	Starts with 'Once upon a time'	Bad magic
Ends 'Happily ever after' or similar	Characters make good choices	Giants and / or monsters	Written in the third person	Uses adverbs

Write your own fairy tale for a younger child. It needs to be a traditional one, like those by Hans Christian Andersen. It should be recognisable as a fairy tale, containing the features seen in this topic.

Step 1: Using the lists of features, choose suitable characters and settings for your story. Try to give the characters romantic, old-fashioned names.

Step 2: The basic plot contains a problem that is created at the start – for example, a curse is put on someone. The remainder of the story is about how the victim comes to solve the problem and learns important lessons in the process. Decide what the problem is going to be at the start and which characters are going to be affected.

Step 3: The victim then has to undergo a series of tests, or go on a journey in order to solve their problem. Decide what those tests are, or what the journey will involve.

Step 4: Before the problem is resolved, the victim has to undergo one last test – they may fail, but then be saved, like Snow White, or they may pass it. Decide what that test is and what the result is. After that, it's quite easy to finish the story, because we know how it will end… happily ever after!

Step 5: Remember to write in the third person and use plenty of adverbs and adjectives to create an appropriate style. After writing it, try reading it to a younger relative to see what reaction you get – based on their reaction, you might wish to redraft and improve it.

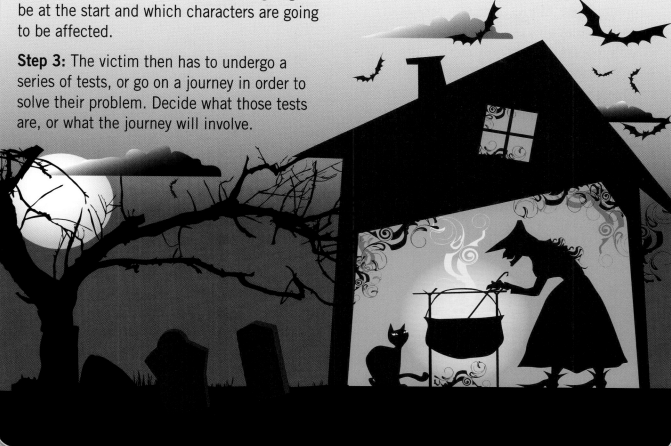

Write a politically-correct fairy tale like James Finn Garner's, or update a traditional story with modern references. For example, you might have Cinderella marrying the lead singer of a boy band and her ugly sisters could be rejects from a reality TV show!

Media Texts

What is Covered in this Topic?

This topic looks at...
- types of media texts
- features of media texts
- the main types of media you may encounter in day-to-day life.

What are Media Texts?

'Media' refers to the ways that ideas are communicated. Media texts can take many forms, for example...
- newspapers, magazines and leaflets
- radio and television programmes
- emails, telephones and text messages
- film posters, websites and maps
- everyday media, such as notes left in the kitchen.

Each of these text types is still affected by the audience you're writing for and the purpose of your writing.

Everyday Printed Media

Each media text can be studied in depth on its own, but there are several main media types you may encounter in everyday life.

Newspapers – Not all newspapers target the same audience:
- **Broadsheets** tend to be more serious and formal.
- **Tabloids** tend to be less serious, and deal with celebrity and entertainment stories more.

A newspaper's purpose is to inform and entertain. Broadsheets tend to inform more, while tabloids tend to entertain.

💡 *Can you name any broadsheet and tabloid newspapers?*

Magazines – Who a magazine is written for varies as there are many **specialist** magazines, all targeting their own specific audience. For example...
- film magazines are written for film-goers
- home improvement magazines are written for people who like DIY.

Like newspapers, a magazine's purpose is to inform and entertain.

Everyday Printed Media (cont.)

Brochures and leaflets – Like magazines, brochures and leaflets cover thousands of subjects and are written to suit specific audiences.

Their purpose is to…
- sell a product and provide information about it
- to provide advice, e.g. a health leaflet.

Adverts – Adverts are written to attract the people the companies hope to sell their products to. Each advert is designed and styled to attract and appeal to its target audience.

The aim is to sell a product. Occasionally they might provide more information, but their main aim is to sell things.

Everyday Electronic Media

Websites – There are as many different types of websites as there are subjects and genres, so it's difficult to say who they're written for and aimed at. Each one needs to be looked at separately, based on its content.

Email – An email is an electronic letter, so there are as many types of email as there are types of letter. There are personal emails, emails of complaint, junk emails – spam, etc.

Text messages – A large proportion of text messages are written for friends or people we know well, so this affects how they're written. For example, shortened slang may be used in a text sent to a friend. Some text messages are sent to advertise or sell products.

Printed Media Example

This is an example of how a newspaper reports a UFO sighting.

It refers to 'readers' and 'phone calls' and uses 'our', which are characteristic of the way newspapers write about, and to, their audience.

BRITAIN is turning into an alien nation, according to readers who have flooded us with reports of UFO sightings.

Following our story of a UFO seen in Stoke-on-Trent, we were inundated with phone calls from people who had seen similar things all over the country.

Some claimed they had seen alien spacecraft over Sneyd Green where our original UFO was snapped.

A man, who asked to be known just as Grant, took a photo of a strangely-shaped object which appeared to be 'buzzing' the local Co-op.

Media Texts

Electronic Media Example

This is an example of how electronic media, such as websites, report news. It refers to a specialist subject and suggests a link to click on.

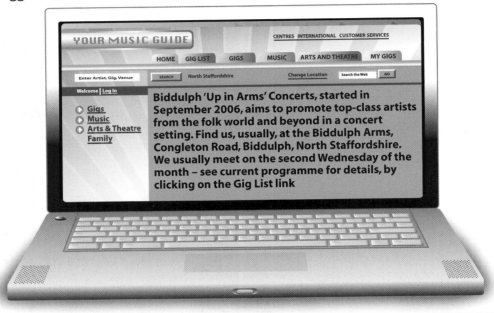

Features of Newspapers

Here is a typical **local** tabloid newspaper's front page:

It contains the following features:
1. Newspaper name – the **masthead**.
2. The regional edition.
3. A guide to what's in the paper.
4. Main news headline.
5. **Teaser** to inside story.
6. Advert.

Features of a Website

A website can contain the following features:

1. Website **banner**.
2. Menu.
3. Teaser for features contained elsewhere on the site.
4. Member access.
5. Introductory **blurb**.
6. Search **facility**.

It has some features similar to the front page of a newspaper – both have a heading to identify the paper or site and both include teasers to get the reader to explore inside.

They might also both have headlines if there's a main story to broadcast.

Quick Test

1. A newspaper is a media text – true or false?
2. A tabloid newspaper is usually less serious than a broadsheet – true or false?
3. Media texts can't be used to entertain – true or false?
4. What is the masthead on a newspaper?
5. What is a teaser on a newspaper?

Media Texts

Key Words Exercise

1 **Are the following key word definitions correct or incorrect?**

a) Broadsheet – A type of newspaper that was originally quite large and is generally more serious in style and content.

b) Tabloid – A type of newspaper that was originally quite large and is generally more serious in style and content.

c) Specialist – A word describing general magazines.

d) Brochure – A type of text often used to display goods or things for sale.

e) Advert – A type of text that persuades people to buy something.

f) Local – Based all over the country.

g) Teaser – A contents list.

h) Masthead – The bottom of a newspaper, where the advert is.

i) Facility – A place where you can find what's on a website.

j) Menu – A list of options or features.

k) Blurb – The back of a newspaper.

l) Banner – Part of a website that often includes information on the purpose of the site.

2 When you have identified which definitions are incorrect, work out the correct definitions.

Are the following statements true or false?

1. 'Media' refers to the ways that ideas are communicated.

2. Sticky notes left in the kitchen are a form of media text.

3. Text messages aren't media texts.

4. Broadsheet newspapers usually contain a lot of celebrity and entertainment gossip.

5. Tabloid newspapers usually contain a lot of celebrity and entertainment gossip.

6. Magazines are often written for specialist audiences.

7. Brochures are only used to sell holidays.

8. Adverts are never used to give information, only to sell.

9. Websites have nothing in common with newspapers.

10. Email stands for 'electronic mail' and is a type of letter.

11. Spam email is a form of media text.

12. Text messages aren't proper media texts because they use slang.

13. Text messages contain slang because we mainly use them to communicate with people we know and who generally understand us.

14. A leaflet is an example of a printed media text.

15. A text message is an example of a printed media text.

16. A text message is an example of an electronic media text.

17. Newspapers often contain small glimpses on the front page of what's inside, in order to get people to buy them.

18. A newspaper masthead is so-called because it's at the top of the front page, like a masthead used to be the top part of a sailing ship.

19. Electronic media texts don't have any features that are different from printed media texts.

20. Printed media texts and electronic media texts can both be interactive with their readers.

Media Texts

Skills Practice

Design a tabloid newspaper's front page. The stories and features to include on the front page are:

- **Main story – Famous celebrity goes missing.**
- **Teaser story – Prime Minister increases teachers' wages by 200%. Picture on front page and few details, full story inside.**
- **Name of paper, edition and date (for you to invent).**
- **Advert for a holiday company.**
- **Other features, which might include teasers for entertainment and celebrity features inside the paper. Look at tabloid newspapers to get ideas.**

Step 1: Decide what your paper is going to be called and which edition and date it will be. Think of a headline for your main story. Use no more than six words so that it's catchy. You might also use a pun or alliteration.

Step 2: Make a sketch plan of the page. Use tabloid-sized paper if it's available. Work out how much space you need for the main story. Estimate how many words or paragraphs you'll be able to fit in.

Step 3: Write the main story. Keep paragraphs short and vocabulary straightforward in order to appeal to the kind of reader you want to attract. Draft your other text on your plan, including the headline.

Step 4: When everything fits, start the final version. If you don't have tabloid-sized paper, you could piece together your newspaper from a number of smaller sheets, like a jigsaw. This is how early newspapers were put together, before computers simplified the process. Computer desktop publishing software would be a good way to piece together and rearrange the page.

Step 5: Compare your newspaper to an actual tabloid – how close is it in style and layout? What might you have done differently to have made it even more realistic?

Extension Activity

Design a website for an up-and-coming band. Include some of the features you have learned to make it attractive and informative.

Speaking and Listening

Transferable Skills

This coursebook focuses on reading and writing skills. However, lots of the skills covered will help you in speaking and listening situations if applied properly, as many of the same ideas apply.

For example, it is important to...
- consider your audience
- use an appropriate style of language, e.g. **Standard English**, local **dialect** or **slang**
- use an appropriate tone of voice
- vary sentence length, **pace** and tone
- use features like irony and similes where appropriate to make it interesting.

Developing Your Speaking and Listening

Speaking and Listening isn't formally assessed by an external examination until the end of KS4, at GCSE. However, it's important to practise in the meantime.

Speaking and Listening skills are developed by working with other people – talking, discussing and sharing ideas in different situations, for example...
- asking questions in class
- answering questions in class
- informal **discussions** (in pairs or groups)
- formal **debate**
- giving a talk (formal or informal)
- reading aloud
- role play or drama.

Whatever the situation, make sure you make a positive contribution:
- Don't just sit in silence and listen.
- Don't talk too much and / or ignore ideas put forward by others.
- Listen and respond to the ideas of others.
- Don't become aggressive.
- Put forward your ideas in a clear and calm manner.

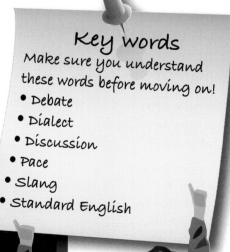

Key words
Make sure you understand these words before moving on!
- Debate
- Dialect
- Discussion
- Pace
- Slang
- Standard English

Glossary and Index

Glossary of Terms in this Book

1st person – writing from the point of view of the person speaking, e.g. 'I walked through the door and up the stairs.' 1st person writing allows the reader to see and experience the thoughts of the writer directly.

3rd person – writing from the point of view of an observer, looking at events from outside, e.g. 'He walked over to the door and opened it. Behind the door stood a table, on which was a letter.' 3rd person writing allows the reader to get an overview of events.

Abstract – something is abstract when it exists, but cannot be seen. It can refer to feelings and emotions, e.g. 'fear' and 'love' exist, but we can't see them.

Clause – this is a part or a section of a sentence. If it is a main clause it will make sense on its own and can also be a sentence, e.g. 'The boy was tall.' A subordinate clause is information added onto the main clause, which adds extra detail. It can come before, after or around the main clause. It does not make sense on its own.

Examples:
- The boy was tall, **(main clause)** because he had a healthy diet **(subordinate clause)**.
- Because he had a healthy diet **(subordinate clause)**, the boy was tall **(main clause)**.
- The boy, because he had a healthy diet, was tall **(main clause split by subordinate clause)**.

Cliché – a word or phrase that's been overused and has lost its original power or meaning, e.g. when footballers say 'I'm sick as a parrot' or 'I'm over the moon.'

Complex sentence – a sentence that contains one independent clause (a main clause that makes sense on its own) and one or more dependent clauses (extra information that relates to the main, independent clause), e.g. 'Because money is tight, we need to spend less.' The first clause doesn't make sense without the second, so this makes it a complex sentence.

Compound sentence – sentence that contains two independent or main clauses, linked by a connective, e.g. 'I like my friend (**1st independent clause**) and my friend likes me (**2nd independent clause**).'

Connectives – words or phrases used to link the different parts of sentences, such as 'and', 'but', 'on the other hand', 'furthermore' and many others.

Interactive – something that allows the reader or viewer to take part, e.g. a website would be interactive if it allowed readers to post comments or upload videos.

Index